PRAISE FOR
The Compassion of

D0340309

"...an extraordinary combination of in..feeling."
— **Cleveland Amory, author of** *Ranch of Dreams*
and *The Cat Who Came for Christmas*

"When next you hear someone accuse another of behaving as 'an animal,' know that an unintended compliment has been offered. *The Compassion of Animals* reveals why."
— **Berkeley Breathed, Pulitzer Prize–winning
cartoonist and author**

"The more I read this book, the more I'm convinced that animals should be elected to high government posts—they're intelligent, honest, courageous, compassionate, and remarkably loyal. And it's almost impossible to corrupt a corgi. Kristin von Kreisler does an outstanding job making the case that dogs, cats, and other non-human animals deserve our respect, protection, and thanks."
— **Mitchell Fox, president,
The Progressive Animal Society (PAWS)**

"The stories Kristin von Kreisler has compiled illustrate the kind-ness of animals. Whether or not there is a scientific understanding for the reasoning behind these acts of kindness, animal lovers know they can count on their animal friends for compassion."
— **Robert Hilsenroth, D.V.M., executive director,
Morris Animal Foundation**

"For about twenty years I've logged news reports of attacks on people by animals and heroic deeds by animals, both wild and domesticated. Surprised that animals have either the effrontery to assault a human or the altruism to save one, people usually describe such incidents as 'unexpected.' Yet animals are often as brave and kindly...as any humans....When humans better understand the courage and generosity of animals, as these accounts collected by Kristin von Kreisler exemplify, they will be...better able to accept the often unrecognized but substantial contributions of animals toward mutual benefit."
— **Merritt Clifton, editor,** *Animal People*

THE COMPASSION OF ANIMALS

KRISTIN VON KREISLER

The
COMPASSION
of ANIMALS

TRUE STORIES OF

ANIMAL COURAGE AND KINDNESS

Prima Publishing

PRIMA PUBLISHING and colophon are registered trademarks of Prima Communications, Inc.

The author took great care to verify that the facts and events in this book are accurate and complete. Every effort was made to contact the people involved in each story, but in some instances, the author had to rely on other sources, such as veterinarians, policemen, eyewitnesses, and written accounts. Although the sources are believed to be reliable, the author and publisher cannot accept responsibility for inaccuracies based on the sources' remarks. If an error was made, please send a correction to Kristin von Kreisler, c/o Prima Publishing, 3875 Atherton Road, Rocklin, California 95765.

Interior design by Trina Stahl
Illustrations by Lisa Cooper

Library of Congress Cataloging-in-Publication Data
von Kreisler, Kristin.
    The compassion of animals : true stories of animal courage and kindness / Kristin von Kreisler.
        p.   cm.
    ISBN 0-7615-0990-9
    1. Altruistic behavior of animals—Anecdotes.   2. Domestic animals—Behavior—Anecdotes.   I. Title.
    QL775.5.V65   1997
    591.5—dc21   97-29900
                                                                       CIP
97 98 99 00 01 HH 10 9 8 7 6 5 4 3 2 1
Printed in the United States of America

How to Order
Single copies may be ordered from Prima Publishing, P.O. Box 1260BK, Rocklin, CA 95677; telephone (916) 632-4400. Quantity discounts are also available. On your letterhead, include information concerning the intended use of the books and the number of books you wish to purchase.

Visit us online at www.primapublishing.com

For John,
whose love and support
have sustained me
for so many years

———

"Three things in . . . life are important.
The first is to be kind. The second is to be kind.
And the third is to be kind."

—HENRY JAMES

CONTENTS

Foreword

UNTIL A very short time ago, if you were to visit a university science library and look up the topic of animal emotions, you would find a series of books on what we term the negative emotions. These would be books about aggression and pain and fear. But you would not find a book about any of the so-called higher emotions, feelings such as love or compassion or sympathy among animals. Now, however, there is a renewed interest in this topic, especially among the younger animal behavior experts. Fran de Waals recently published *Good Natured* about friendship and cooperation among chimpanzees. But the subject of compassion, especially compassion across species, still seems taboo.

It had been widely believed for centuries that no other animal besides human beings could display genuine compassion even for another of its own species, let alone for a member of a different species. And yet there are more and more anecdotes (and when there are enough of these, they cease to be mere anecdotes and deserve the more dignified name of data) about animals that show what looks very much like compassion. The book you are about to read is one of the first collections of these stories to appear. One of the few stories I have heard about that is not included in this collection comes from a quite accidental videotape of a hippopotamus who saved a small gazelle from a Nile crocodile. When the injured calf was struggling to stand up, the hippo stood over it protectively and opened its giant mouth to breathe warm breath onto the small animal, in the hopes of reviving it. It did this not once, but five times, before giving up. Animal behaviorists who viewed the video were puzzled. Using the ordinary scientific paradigm, they were simply unable to account for the hippo's actions, for these fell outside any of the normal categories they were accustomed to applying. How could a hippo endanger itself in order to save a member of another species? There seemed to be no survival value in such altruism. What possible benefit could it derive? That the hippo was not engaged in a cost/benefit analysis and was just showing the other animal simple compassion was evidently beyond the scientific imagination.

Recently, the world was electrified by a story that you will read about in this book, of a three-year-old boy who fell eighteen feet onto concrete in a gorilla exhibit at the Brookfield Zoo in Chicago. Binti, a seven-year-old female with a baby gorilla on her back, picked up the child, cradled him in her arms, and placed him near a door where keepers could retrieve him. The child survived with no permanent injuries. Why was this clip, flashed across television screens around the world, so affecting? Why are so many people moved to tears by such images? Another story you will read about here took place in December 1995, when a feral domestic cat squeezed through a hole in a fence that corrals a 560-pound bear at Wildlife Images, a wildlife rehabilitation center in Grants Pass, Oregon. The cat approached the bear as he was eating from a five-gallon bucket. So hungry was the cat that he was seen to walk up to the bear and beg for food. Dave Siddon, founder of the center, thought the bear would kill the cat. Instead, the bear pulled a little piece of chicken out and dropped it beside his forepaw, and watched the cat walk up and eat it. Afterward, the cat and the bear remained together—eating, sleeping, and romping round the pen—the best of friends. People are now flocking to the center merely to observe the two friends together.

There are more and more such stories being reported around the world. Are such acts of clear compassion becoming more frequent in the animal kingdom? I think a far more likely explanation is that we, as a species, are beginning at last to allow other animals to feel emotions we thought unique to humans and, in fact, are relieved, even delighted, to find this to be the case. Kristin von Kreisler tells us about many of these acts of compassion. Thinking about these wonderful stories led me to consider that feeling compassion and committing compassionate acts make sense from an evolutionary point of view. Solitary animals—cats, for example—do not need to show compassion to survive, and examples of compassion among the big cats are scarce (which does not mean they never happen). (Domestic cats, on the other hand, as the stories in this book illustrate, are another matter entirely.)

Nevertheless, humans and other social animals must learn to get on with one another to survive. As Auden wrote: "We must love one another or die." It is odd to realize that there are far more, and far better, studies of the *lack* of compassion than of its existence. We are more knowledgeable about the failure of empathy than we are about the conditions necessary for it to thrive. There is a paradoxical truth involved: We can be certain that the Kitty Genovese syndrome is what it appears to be. People do fail to help one another, of that there can be no doubt. But when somebody proves a hero of compassion, we are reluctant to believe it, especially in this age of fallen heroes, without more proof. Albert Schweitzer was not the man we thought he was; could it be that Raoul Wallenberg had a dark side? The literature on the rescuers, as opposed to the murderers, of Jews is still meager. We understand the positive emotions much less than we do the negative ones.

The animal that lives in a community learns the value of helping another individual. Rats are reluctant to press a lever to get food if doing so will also deliver an electric shock to a companion. They will invariably press the lever that will not deliver the shock, and some will even forego food rather than hurt their friends. Maybe that is why rats make good companions, why *rattus Norvegicus* can be so affectionate with children. These experiments with rats embarrassed the scientists who conducted them. They did not expect to find evidence of compassion among rodents.

We all know what happened when Stanley Milgram asked graduate students at Yale to deliver potentially lethal shocks to subjects in a diabolical experiment he conducted to simulate what was happening in the Eichmann trial in Jerusalem. His results were painful for all to see: Most undergraduates were only too willing to deliver the shock if they were told to do so by someone they perceived to be in authority. Where does this lack of compassion come from? Have we strayed further from a more natural inclination to help than is healthy for our species, or are we just following our pre-programmed nature?

The nature/nurture debate can take on a new dimension if we examine the compassionate side of our evolutionary cousins. Until now, it has been difficult to find all the stories one needs to consider gathered together in one convenient place. Kristin von Kreisler's book does just that and provides more evidence that we humans, as a species, have something important to learn from other animals. It will also delight the reader—who can ever get enough stories of animals that ignore their own welfare to help their friends, to help us, to help other animals, and even to help complete strangers? I defy any reader to get to the end of this book without shedding tears—tears of sadness at the terrible acts humans have committed against animals, but also tears of delight at the marvelous courage and compassion displayed by dogs, cats, horses, and other animals.

I finished reading this book with the thought that it is becoming increasingly clear that we still know very little about animals who have lived with us for thousands of years. It is time we stopped comparing ourselves to other animals (in the hopes of always coming out on top) and instead simply listen, in awe, to stories that remind us how much we are part of a greater chain of being. This book will help you to remember some of the feelings you had as a child for the animals to whom you were closest. Those feelings had everything to do with compassion. That is what this book is all about.

—Jeffrey Moussaieff Masson, Ph.D.,
author of *Dogs Never Lie About Love*
and co-author of *When Elephants Weep*

ACKNOWLEDGMENTS

THE COMPASSION of many people lies behind this book. I could never have written it without the help and support of all those who let me interview them about their animals or who found me stories of animal kindness.

I especially thank Merrit Clifton, editor of *Animal People;* Lee Rammage at Ralston Purina Canada Inc.; Jessie Vicha and Tom O'Brien at Ken-L Ration Dog Foods; Carol Moulton and Betty A. Lewis at the American Humane Association; Linda Hines and Leo Bustad at the Delta Society; Janice Rooney at the Morris Animal Foundation; John Becker at the Texas Veterinary Medical Association; Richard Alampi at the New Jersey Veterinary Medical Association; Glenn Kolb at the Oregon Veterinary Medical Association; Mary Wamsley at the Los Angeles S.P.C.A.; Cheryl Conway at the Animal Care Division of Aurora, Colorado; Matt Kleinman at *Unsolved Mysteries;* and my friends Kay Podolsky and Becky Cooper.

I also thank my agent, Julian Bach, for his interest and encouragement, and my editors, Susan Silva and Jennifer Fox, for their careful handling of this project.

I thank wonderful friends who contributed to this book by boosting my spirits or helping me write. Martha Hannon was, as always, my mentor and guide; Clell Bryant gave his excellent editorial advice; Bonnie Remsberg offered her wisdom.

INTRODUCTION

ONE OF the best parts of being a writer is that I can work in my office all day surrounded by my pets. Tigger, my tabby kitty, drapes herself across the Morris chair and makes occasional tiny squeaks that sound like air escaping from a tire. Ludwig, who looks like a distinguished gentleman disguised in a stunning German shepherd suit, lies in a patch of sun beneath my skylight and fills the room with manly snores.

And then there's Bea. I found her, a scrawny, frantic beagle, on the road near my house. A later inspection revealed a tattoo in her ear, and I discovered that she had escaped from a medical lab. With her legs flopped out, she sprawls on her back on the oriental rug, makes muffled yips, and pedals her feet. She dreams, I suppose, of chasing rabbits. After the "hunt," she rolls on her side and assumes the shape of a lima bean. The snuffles from the sides of her mouth sound like fingers rubbing a balloon.

These sighs and snores, a gentle background for my work, continue all day. The animals are as much a part of my office as my computer is, but they keep their distance and are busy with their naps. When I write, Bea, Tigger, and Ludwig do not bother me.

That is, they didn't bother me until one hot Indian-summer day—October 18, 1989. The sultry San Francisco Bay Area weather made me and the animals restless and grouchy. They lay around the room in heaps, then got up, their little nails clicking on the hardwood as they padded to the bathroom and sought the cool relief of a tile floor. Ludwig, panting, shifted repeatedly in his sleeping spot. Bea wanted to be let out, then in, then out again.

After I let her in yet another time and returned to my desk, the house shook violently. The motion knocked me out of my chair and slammed me against a file cabinet. A painting fell off the wall. When a lamp crashed to the floor, I knew I had to run.

We were having an earthquake—not just a few unsettling tremors, but a roller-coaster ride that felt like hanging onto a brontosaurus wrestling with his brother. My animals had apparently sensed this coming. As I dashed to the back door, they skidded across the floor behind me. The ground shuddered and threw us against the walls with a thud. With difficulty, I unlocked the door and pulled it open.

We ran for our lives. Tigger disappeared into the forest. Ludwig, clearly wanting to get as far as possible from our dangerous house, raced to the gate. Bea, who seemed more terrified and confused than any of us, tore halfway up the hill next to the vegetable garden and plastered herself against the fence—perhaps hoping to push her way through it and escape.

My knees knocked together so uncontrollably that I sat on a tree stump to keep from falling. I tried to calm myself as I watched the redwoods sway over my house. I prayed they would not topple onto the roof—and the house would not collapse into a pile of rubble.

In San Francisco, houses *did* collapse. A piece of the Bay Bridge even fell into the water. And calling 911 often brought no help. To make matters even more unbearable, Dan Rather kept tormenting residents by reminding them that the earthquake was not "The Big One," in spite of being 7.1 on the Richter scale: We had worse in store for us in the days ahead.

Still, at the time I knew none of this. My electricity and telephone were out, and I had no way of reaching the outside world. My husband was away on business in southern California. I had no close neighbors. In other words, I could have screamed forever, and no one would have heard me. I was living out my greatest childhood fear: being in a desperate situation, terrified and starkly, irreversibly, alone.

I sat on my tree stump until the brontosaurus seemed to make peace with his brother. Then I gathered my courage, went into the house, and filled the bathtub with water in case aftershocks broke the pipes. With a wrench I tried to turn off the gas but could not tell if I'd succeeded. While I picked up books that had fallen from their shelves, I looked for damage. (Only one new crack had appeared in the mortar between the fireplace bricks.) My knees kept knocking as I went about my tasks, and every few minutes I ran outside just to stand in the open and reassure myself.

By evening the animals came to the patio and ate the dinners I had set out for them. For myself, I heated tomato soup on the camper stove. Because I felt too afraid to eat or sleep indoors, I placed a rubber mattress and sleeping bag on the patio, well away from any trees and walls that could tumble down. I placed Bea's and Ludwig's pillows close to my bed and climbed, fully clothed, into the unzipped bag—the better to run in an emergency. Tigger perched on the wall bordering the patio. The dogs plumped themselves up on their pillows.

As I closed my eyes, the ground rumbled with aftershocks, but I told myself over and over to count my blessings. The animals and I were safe. The house could have been destroyed, but it was fine. Even so, I continued to tremble so deeply inside that my bone marrow seemed to slosh around in little waves.

My mind filled with images of looters, who were surely roaming the streets that very minute looking for a house in which a woman would be alone, defenseless. They would break down the front door, kill my pets, carry off my grandmother's silver pitcher, and then, dear God, do unspeakable things to me. I would lie helpless on the patio, bleeding profusely from my wounds, while the men escaped in their car. I could never say good-bye to my husband, who would return from his trip to find vultures feasting on my entrails.

To defend myself against my imagination, I opened my eyes and watched the lovely, silver moon. I wrapped my arms around my body for security and told myself I wasn't alone: God was with me. I prayed for calm. Yet I could not be at peace—the terror of the earthquake was still too recent. I couldn't remember ever feeling so alone.

Then Tigger wandered over from her perching spot, butted her chin against my cheek, and settled in the crook behind my knees. Ludwig left his pillow, lay down on the patio, and curled his body protectively around my head. And Bea—who had been so abused that I'd had to teach her what love was—shoved her nose under the cover and rooted into the sleeping bag. She pressed against my chest, rested her head on my neck, and cuddled up. Her gentle, meaty breaths warmed my skin.

I was certain that my pets were worried about me and wanted to help. I knew right down to those waves in my bone marrow that the animals had not come to *get* comfort but to *give* it. They wanted to be sure I was all right.

As we huddled together, I felt safe. The comfort my animals offered seemed different from their normal daily affection. That night their comforting was spiritual, an epiphany for me, one of the a-ha! moments that Fritz Perls described, when people suddenly understand something and are never the same again. I realized that I could give up my childhood fear: As long as I had pets who clearly cared so much about me, no matter what happened, I would never be alone. I might be traumatized, as I had been that day, but if my animals were there, I would have all I needed to get through what was asked of me. The Lord provided—in the form of warm, furry bodies that encased noble spirits. That truth was so simple, yet so profound.

A FEW days later, still contemplating this experience, I learned that a dog in Watsonville (about an hour's drive from my house) might have given a young girl at least a child's understanding of this truth during the earth-quake. The dog was Reeona, a two-and-a-half-year-old rottweiler. As a puppy, she had been so abused that when she was finally adopted into a new home, no one was able to touch her for a week. After the dog felt the earth jolt and heard screams from the house across the street, she tore out the door. She jumped three fences—something she'd never attempted before—and bounded into the neighbor's house, where she found five-year-old Vivian Cooper, terrified and screaming in the kitchen.

Reeona shoved the child against a cabinet and, with 102 pounds of her furry body, sat on the girl to keep her still. Seconds later, vibrations moved a heavy microwave oven from the top of the refrigerator. The oven crashed to the floor on the very spot where Vivian had been standing. Even though the little girl barely knew the dog and had always been frightened of her, she hugged Reeona, buried her face in the dog's fur, and clung to her while they rode out the quake. Reeona protected and calmed Vivian—and the dog's soothing presence kept the girl from having one of the seizures that often occurred when she got scared.

THE ORDEAL of the earthquake made me realize what I suppose I've always known, yet had not felt so deeply and with such conviction: Animals are capable of great kindness and compassion; they rescue, comfort, and care for us. They are one of life's great blessings.

Unfortunately, many people don't regard animals in this way. Not far from where I live, a large university and many corporations have laboratories where researchers experiment on animals. I am greatly troubled that creatures are being harmed anywhere—especially so near to my own house. Sometimes I imagine them cramped in cages, malnourished, and subjected to painful procedures, as my beagle had been. If I think too much about all the abused animals in the world, especially knowing how sensitive animals can be and how great their capacity for kindness, I nearly drive myself crazy.

In the months following the earthquake, I asked myself: How can I help these animals? And the answer that came to me was: I can write about how compassionate and full of heart animals can be. I can describe their kindness to me and Vivian Cooper, and I can tell the stories of other caring creatures.

I combed through magazines and newspapers, contacted animal organizations, and searched the Internet for several months in order to find those stories. I was stunned by the huge number I discovered—accounts of both domestic and captive animals giving everything they had to help others. If I'd kept searching, I could have easily found thousands more.

These stories, of animals dragging people from fires or towing them to shore, didn't just turn up randomly or occasionally. They were everywhere. Animals showed concern for others all the time, all over the world, in every sort of circumstance and condition. Stray dogs appeared out of nowhere and risked their lives to carry out rescues. Creatures with homes came to the aid of people they'd never even seen before.

And animals saved other animals, sometimes not even members of their own species. I read about a cat who protected a fish, a dog who foster-parented hedgehogs, and a cow who got help for a dog that was buried alive. And I discovered tales about every species of helpful creature—not just cats and dogs and cows, but also pigs, horses, bears, gorillas, dolphins, and even an iguana.

These animals showed great ingenuity in carrying out their generous deeds. Without hands or speech, the animals managed to give first aid, deliver messages and warnings, get help, offer comfort, and transport to safety people who often weighed twice as much as the animals themselves. In the process, the animals frequently got sick, lost, mangled, or abused. They pitted themselves against seemingly impossible odds or took the hit for someone in trouble. The animals seemed willing to endure whatever was necessary in order to carry out their missions. In fact, many animals even gave their lives.

I wondered what these creatures were feeling when they acted with such loyalty and kindness, and to find out, I contacted evolutionary biologists, veterinarians, animal behaviorists, and zoologists. I told them about the stories I'd collected and asked how these animals' actions could be explained. Now, instead of being stunned merely by the huge number of accounts, I was also stunned by the experts' opinions.

According to all but one of the researchers, animals are not capable of compassion. Yet animals, through their own deeds, tell us otherwise. Perhaps we should reconsider, with an open mind, the evidence the animals present to us with their own actions.

CHAPTER ONE

ATTUNED *to* DANGER

C OLLIN STOLPES drove away from his Oregon home, so bitter and angry that he wanted to die. He had lost his farm and business—the way he figured it, he'd been *cheated* out of them. Now he was homeless; everything he and his wife, Deb, owned was packed into their forty-passenger transit bus, along with their mutt Tiger.

About an hour after crossing the Oregon state line, Deb got up from her seat, walked to the back of the bus, and returned with a shoe box. Collin, in the driver's seat, kept his eyes on the road until she laid the box on his lap.

He lifted the lid. Out poked a black-and-white head. Two tiny ears. Two black eyes. A small pink snout.

"We can't keep this pig!" Collin snapped.

"It's too late to turn around and bring her back," Deb pleaded. She loved the pig. She loved all animals.

Grudgingly, Collin lifted the pig from its box. As he drove on, she fell asleep in his hand. She appeared to be as lost and vulnerable as he felt. She needed protection.

The pig was part of a litter that had been born on the farm just two days earlier. While Collin had packed, Deb had begged to bring her along. He'd refused, insisting that he had enough trouble: A pig was just one more thing to worry about and the last thing he needed. Now, though, taking her back would mean he'd have to see the farm again. Besides wasting time, returning there would upset him even more.

"You win," Collin conceded.

His thoughts were dark. Everything in his life seemed out of control and could only get worse. He had to get away from Oregon and everything it represented—yet he had no idea where to go. More depressed than he'd ever been in his life, he headed south, along with Deb, Tiger, and the pig, whom they named Snort. And for the next four months, they camped and fished and hiked and drifted.

Snort soon grew from a piglet to a thirty-pound creature the size of a bulldog. The fuzz on her black-and-white skin turned to bristles. Her tail, which she wagged constantly, grew to six inches long.

The pig also became Deb's beloved pet, flipping on her back for belly rubs and nibbling Deb's toes to demand attention. Deb painted her hooves with dainty pink nail polish and cut ear holes in Collin's baseball caps for her to wear. Deb also convinced Collin to cut a special door in the front of the bus, so Snort could come and go at night. Collin added a ramp to the ground; they called it "Snort's speedway."

The pig used her "speedway" until one windy October night in Aurora, Colorado, where Deb and Collin had parked the bus in front of his sister Claudia's house. In order to keep warm in the below-zero temperature, they pulled up Snort's ramp and closed her door, as well as the windows to the bus.

After getting Snort and Tiger settled in their sleeping spots, Collin turned on the built-in propane heater and climbed into bed. A cold wind rattled the bus and made the night seem bleak and lonely. Collin and Deb fell asleep, but Snort did not. She rooted around in her bed and acted anxious, distressed. A few hours later she raced down the aisle of the bus and oinked so loudly that she woke Deb.

Thinking that Snort wanted to relieve herself, Deb took her outside. In the moonlight, Snort calmed down but still refused to be quiet. She walked around, sniffed Claudia's lawn—but showed absolutely no interest in doing what Deb had brought her out to do. Puzzled by the pig's odd behavior, Deb carried her back to the bus and got into bed.

But not for long. This time, even more adamant about waking her family, Snort thrashed her portly body around the bus and oinked and snorted in alarm. She would not be quiet no matter what Deb did to hush her. Finally, Deb dragged her outside again. Yet Snort was still not satisfied. She circled around, rustled in the dry grass, and seemed to be trying to communicate something to Deb. Shivering in the wind, Deb wrapped her arms around herself and breathed in the cold air. Had Snort gone crazy? She had always been a docile, cheerful pig. Now look at her: She was behaving like a hyperactive maniac. She also clearly had no intention of going to the bathroom.

"Go! Potty! Do it!" Deb urged Snort.

Snort would not. Frustrated, Deb herded her back into the bus.

Snort was still upset. By 5 A.M. she had worked herself into a frenzy. She squealed, tore up and down the aisle, and made so much noise that Tiger growled at her. Deb bolted up in bed.

"*You* take her out this time," she demanded of Collin.

Collin didn't answer. In the dark, she squinted at him and shook his shoulder. "Collin?" Still no answer. *"Collin."*

At last he managed to gasp, "I can't breathe. I think I'm having a heart attack." Desperately nauseous, he felt that the wind had been knocked out of him. His arms and legs seemed paralyzed. Weak and confused, he was terrified at the sudden unexplained symptoms.

Snort, however, seemed to understand what was going on and treated it as a crisis; nearly hysterical, she shrieked and threw herself around the bus. Deb tossed back the bedcovers and raced across the lawn to Claudia's house. She tried to dial 911, but she couldn't move her fingers; Claudia had to make the call for her.

They ran back to Collin, who was in convulsions. Snort was still squealing and thrashing about, clearly trying to convey that something terrible was happening. Claudia dragged Collin outside to the yard, and Deb and Tiger followed. With everyone finally out of the bus, Snort's panic subsided. Her warning heeded at last, she lay on the ground near Collin and watched him until the ambulance arrived.

In the emergency room, doctors gave Collin oxygen and checked his heart while Deb, whose hands still would not function, tried to fill out the hospital's admission form. She sat there, confused and frightened.

The doctors were confused as well: Collin's heart was fine. Then someone asked if he might have been poisoned by carbon monoxide. And Collin remembered the propane heater. The doctors ran for Deb, who was still woozy and trying to write.

Slowly, the hospital staff pieced together what had happened. The propane heater in the bus had been leaking. By taking Snort outside, Deb had breathed enough fresh air to keep her from getting as sick as Collin. Snort and Tiger, lying on the floor, had also inhaled less carbon monoxide than Collin had.

Snort's exquisite sense of smell—as refined as that of her truffle-hunting European relatives—had enabled her to detect the carbon monoxide almost as soon as Collin had closed up the bus. She'd understood that something was seriously wrong and had been so insistent in her distress that Deb could not ignore her. Without Snort's determination, the doctors said, in just fifteen more minutes Collin would have died.

As Collin slowly recuperated in the hospital, he thought about how much he'd wanted to die after losing his farm and how glad he was now to be alive. Snort's rescue had given him a second chance; he must not waste it by continuing to grieve and mope and nurse his anger. Again and again, he asked himself, "Why didn't I die?" To have had his life saved by a pig—even a pig as sterling as Snort—well, that was crazy. God must be trying to tell me something, Collin decided.

Over the next few weeks, he also decided that he must still be alive for a reason. And he alone would have to figure out what that reason *was*. He prayed, stared into space, and pondered. Gradually, his pessimistic attitude shifted. One morning he loaded Deb, Tiger, and Snort onto the bus and headed to Sioux City, Iowa, in order to start a new life where his adult sons lived.

Working as a truck mechanic, he saved enough money to open a storage business. He also tried to be a better father to his sons. And, of course, he did not forget his obligations to his pig. He built her—weighing 110 pounds by that time—her own personal shed behind his house, and now he proudly walks her, on a leash, around the neighborhood, and he waves and smiles at friendly passersby.

Snort saved more than Collin's life. With her kind heart, she also saved his soul. And even though he can laugh today about the night he almost died, Collin remains profoundly grateful to a pig.

CHAPTER TWO

AGAINST
ALL ODDS

AFTER KATHLEEN FORNATARO finished cleaning her house in Rosenhayn, New Jersey, she sank into her swivel rocker and flipped on the television. She had a few minutes to rest before her husband, Al, came home from work.

Curled in a tiny red ball on the living room carpet was Ginger, her five-pound Pomeranian. Ginger had once been a sprightly little creature who could dance on her hind legs, crawl across the floor on her belly, and perform many other entertaining tricks. Now, however, at age fifteen, she was a nearly toothless geriatric whose dancing days were over. Because of congestive heart disease, she often fell asleep while sitting up and then toppled over. She slept most of the day and, deaf, was oblivious to doorbells and voices.

Fornataro glanced at Ginger to make sure she was still all right, then changed the television channel. At that instant, she heard someone walk, singing, through her front door. She turned her swivel chair to greet the person she thought was her son.

But the wild-eyed man in her living room was *not* her son. He was a huge, menacing stranger with muscles bulging under his shirt. He seemed jittery, like a reed in wind, and swaggered across the room as if he owned the house.

"I know who YOU are!" he screamed. "You're a policeman's wife!"

"No. No, I'm not." Fornataro tried to make her voice sound calm. "My husband isn't a policeman."

The man stepped closer, so overwrought that his whole body shook. "I don't really care if he's a policeman or not! He's dead! Outside! I just killed him! I'M GOING TO KILL YOU NEXT!!"

Instead of coming after her, though, he sat, trembling and twitching, on a chair across the room.

Fornataro's heart was beating so hard that it felt as if a panic-stricken animal were trapped inside her ribs. Waves of nausea rippled through her stomach. Her saliva tasted of fear. Now she was certain that Al had driven up and pulled into the garage, where this maniac had killed him. In her mind she pictured Al stabbed, bleeding, and slumped over his steering wheel.

Any minute, she'd be dead as well. And so would Ginger, her beloved dog, if she woke and moved from her spot on the floor. Although Ginger was too tiny and decrepit to frighten a normal person, she might make the deranged man even more crazed. He would think nothing of killing her.

For what seemed like millennia, he babbled an inco-
herent string of threats at Fornataro. His cheeks were
flushed as he ranted and yelled. When he stood up, so
did she, in self-defense. He crossed the room and thrust
his sweaty face in hers.

"All right. I'm going to kill you! YOU'RE GOING TO
DIE NOW! NOW!!"

Her head spinning, Fornataro gripped the back of
her rocker.

Then Ginger opened her eyes. She seemed immediately to recognize that the man was dangerous and, yipping and yowling, jumped to her feet. She charged, on
stiff, arthritic legs, across the living room, flung her tiny
body at the huge man, and gummed his ankle. Yelling,
he swung his leg away and kicked her, like a football,
through the air.

Ginger hit the wall and, shrieking in pain, flopped to
the floor. Fornataro ran to her, picked her up, and cradled the dog against her pounding heart. Still certain
that the man was going to kill her, Fornataro whirled
around to face him.

But somehow the ancient little dog's attack had
jarred his thoughts away from murder.

"I'M GOD!" he yelled.

"Yes, sure. Of course, you are."

"You don't believe me, do you?"

"Yes. Yes. I believe you. You're God."

"I can prove it. LOOK!!" The man unbuttoned his
shirt, shoved his naked chest toward Fornataro, then ran
out the front door.

Fornataro, still trembling, rushed to the telephone to call the police. As she dialed, she glanced out the window and saw that patrol cars were already parked in front of her house.

Sobbing, she dashed to the front door. "Find my husband. Please. Please find him," she begged the policemen. "The man has killed him."

But Al's truck was not in the driveway. He had not come home yet. He was still alive.

Relief washed over Fornataro, and she hugged Ginger closer. The brave little dog had saved her. And Al's being late that night had saved him.

The policemen had already been searching her yard with flashlights, looking for a man who'd knocked over a deli's cash register, attacked four people in a parking lot, and run, screaming that he was God, into Fornataro's neighborhood. He was a schizophrenic who had stopped taking the medicine that would control his illness and was so strong and so agitated that it took five policemen to knock him down.

Nevertheless, Ginger—despite being aged, infirm, and toothless—had not hesitated to tackle the six-foot man with her five-pound body in order to protect Fornataro.

TO HELP people they care about, animals will often fight against insurmountable odds. The creatures ignore their size, afflictions, limitations, and safety. All that seems to matter is offering protection, no matter the consequences.

One example of this selfless bravery was published in *Animal Heroes* by Karleen Bradford. Grizzly, a black-and-silver Siberian husky, was the lead dog in the team of Paul Guitard. One June morning he hitched Grizzly and seven other dogs to his four-wheel vehicle and drove them down a trail in Ontario, Canada. Along the way, they accidentally passed between a mother bear and her cubs, and the bear, protective of her babies, lumbered after Guitard. She tugged him away from his team, bit his leg and arm, and dragged him off to kill him.

Usually, if Guitard got separated from his dogs, they kept running. But Grizzly seemed to understand that Guitard was desperate for help. Somehow, Grizzly stopped the other seven dogs and made them turn around. As a team, they all raced back to Guitard.

Despite being harnessed to the seven other dogs, Grizzly leaped on the bear and fought her long enough for Guitard to run away and climb a tree. When the bear realized that her prey had escaped, she chased Guitard, grabbed his foot, and tried to yank him down. He kicked and kicked her. The dog attacked again with such fury that the bear let Guitard go.

Bleeding profusely and blanching with pain, he clung to tree branches for seven hours. Nearly every twenty minutes, the bear returned and tried to reach him. Each time, Guitard braced himself for being torn to pieces. Yet each time, Grizzly fought off the bear. His movements restricted by being harnessed to the team, the dog was as handicapped as a boxer with one hand tied behind his back. Still, he snarled, snapped, and lunged at the bear—and managed to chase her away again and again.

Finally, that afternoon Guitard's friends came down the trail looking for him. As the bear charged, one of the men shot her. They took Guitard to a hospital, where doctors stitched up his wounds. The dog's only injury was a gash that the bear had clawed in his nose.

ON A freezing winter day, Sean Lingl and his friend Danny Parker rowed a small plastic dinghy across the mouth of the Nimpkish River on British Columbia's Vancouver Island. Rain poured down, and wind roughened the water, tossing the dinghy about as if it were a thimble. But the men, eager to get to an island just off the coast, kept rowing.

Lingl's chocolate Labrador retriever Tia sat shivering in the boat between them. Not immediately obvious from the angle of her sitting position was the harsh reality that she had only three legs. Four years before, as she'd chased Lingl's truck down a gravel road, she'd run into a ditch and cut her right hind paw on a broken bottle. Her veterinarian treated the injury, but infection set in and spread up her leg.

"I'll have to amputate it," the vet told Lingl. "I have no choice."

Lingl thought of putting her down. He did not want her hobbling, crippled, through life, with people wincing and pitying her. But the vet persuaded him to let Tia have the surgery. Afterward, her indomitable spirit convinced Lingl that he had been right to let her live.

As the wind blasted water into the dingy, Lingl did not worry. The boat's double plastic hull created a pocket of air that would hold the boat up, no matter how much water filled it, he told Parker. They were in no danger unless a hole was somehow punctured in the outer layer. A hole would let water into the pocket and sink the boat.

When they began tilting farther and farther to one side, however, Lingl did start to worry. "Something's not right," he said. "Maybe we should go back."

"Let's do it," Parker agreed.

As they turned the boat around and headed toward shore, the wind flipped the dinghy over and threw them, along with Tia, into the icy water. The men sputtered, shivering violently. To keep their heads above water, they clung to the side of the capsized boat.

"Where's Tia?" Lingl shouted.

He groped for her and found her trapped under the dinghy. Grabbing her by the fur, he pulled her out and set her free. Even with only three legs, at least she'd have the chance to swim ashore and save herself.

Lingl and Parker were not going to be so lucky. The cold itself was cause for alarm: They could not survive in this water for long. Even worse, they both were wearing heavy boots and chest waders, firmly attached by belts and suspenders. If the waders continued filling with water, Lingl and Parker would sink like anchors. And there was no help in sight.

Lingl pulled himself up just enough to see over the boat. He figured that they had to cross about a hundred yards of freezing waves to reach shore . . . and only a few minutes to do it before they sank or died from exposure. They were looking death in the face, and they knew it.

Then Lingl suddenly noticed that the boat was moving toward the beach. Amazed, he looked around to discover the source of this miraculous motion. Tia had gripped the dinghy's mooring rope between her teeth and, with her three legs, was swimming with every ounce of her strength and pulling the boat to safety.

Astounded by her courage, Lingl and Parker helped her move the boat along by kicking even in their chest waders. Though the wind slapped huge waves in the water and tossed Tia as if she were a cork, she gritted her teeth around the rope and paddled as hard as she could to keep from going under. Blinking against the stinging salt, she battled the waves until she'd pulled Lingl and Parker to water shallow enough for them to stand. She let go of the rope as they staggered to shore.

The men's hair turned instantly to ice as they walked toward the car. Icicles also hung from Tia's fur, but she ignored them. She tottered along with Lingl and Parker as if the day were warm and she'd done nothing special.

Lingl leaned down, hugged her, and thanked her for rescuing them. Any dog towing a boat in freezing, turbulent water was hard to imagine, but a three-legged dog? A three-legged dog who actually succeeded in getting the boat to shore?

"No one will ever believe this," Lingl told Parker.

CHAPTER THREE

CHAMPIONS
of the SICK

GOLIATH, a four-foot-long emerald-green iguana with skin the texture of a football, nestled under Duane Wright's chin in Tucson, Arizona. He murmured to the reptile, whom he'd named Goliath before he realized that she was female, "You're my good girl. I love you!"

Goliath snuggled closer against his neck as if to say, "I love you back." Or at least that's what Wright felt she was conveying.

This exchange was not their only way of showing affection. When Goliath first came to live with Wright, she sneezed.

"I love you, too!" He patted her.

Soon she crawled on his shoulder many times a day and sneezed in his face, he believed, to express her tender feelings for him. For hours she lay across his chest, stretched out her arms, and rested her cheek against his shirt as if she were trying to hug him.

"Iguanas are extremely loving if you love them," Wright told his wife, Arlene.

Goliath, who had fiery brown eyes and sharp little claws, was Wright's companion twenty-four hours a day, seven days a week. She was the only fur-and-dander-free pet that doctors allowed him. Because of his asthma, chronic lung diseases, and severe apnea, Wright was confined most of the time to one room of his house, near machines administering lung medication every few hours and controlling humidity and temperature. During the day, he lay on his bed or recliner with Goliath tucked close. At night he and Goliath slept near an intercom, so that Arlene could monitor his breathing from another room.

One evening Wright wasn't feeling well. Instead of taking Goliath to bed as usual, he tried to dislodge her from his chest and put her on the special stand he'd created from a computer desk. The stand had all of the comforts that he imagined an iguana would appreciate: branches for her to climb in, little pillows and a heating pad to lie on, and even a water bowl, made from a kidney-shaped hospital spittoon, which Wright had covered with plaster of paris and painted black to resemble a rock, so that she'd feel at home.

That night Goliath would have nothing to do with her special perching place. She wouldn't loosen her claws from Wright's shirt and let him go to bed alone. Instead, she insisted on accompanying him and cuddled up across his chest in her usual spot. He patted her, settled under his blanket, and fell asleep.

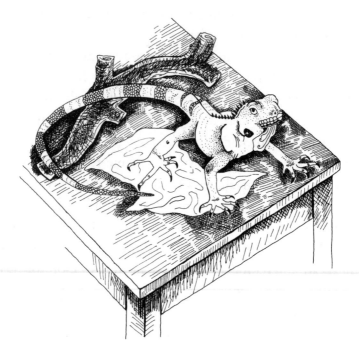

About 1:30 in the morning, he vaguely sensed that Goliath was whipping his face with her tail. But Wright was too sleepy to respond. When he didn't open his eyes, she clawed and bit his face. She was clearly determined to rouse him. As he slept on, she whipped and clawed and made such a fuss that Arlene finally heard her on the intercom.

Arlene hurried to Wright's room to find out what the disturbance was. Just as she entered, Goliath finally succeeded in awakening him. Choking for air, he had stopped breathing. (The iguana may have sensed this coming before Wright had even gone to bed.)

As Goliath watched, her mission accomplished, Arlene helped Wright to a respirator. When his breathing improved, she took him, sick and woozy, to the hospital, where doctors administered oxygen and intravenous prednisone, which cleared his lungs.

Wright told the doctors that Goliath had rescued him; she'd been concerned about him. "You can't help but love an animal that saves your life," he said.

Eager to see his protective iguana, Wright returned home to find Goliath resting on her branch on the computer desk, her green tail hanging in the spittoon water bowl. She was waiting for him.

WHEN PEOPLE experience medical emergencies, animals often become extremely upset and try to find someone to help. Once a woman was awakened by her deaf-mute cat, who, instead of meowing, had begun throwing herself on the woman's chest again and again. The woman discovered that her husband was unconscious and had just had a heart attack.

Brat, a cat in Wheeling, Illinois, woke Karen Ybarra Hummerlich from a sound sleep by licking her eyelids, scratching her, and meowing. When she shooed the cat away, Brat ran to the bedroom door of Hummerlich's son Jose and meowed with such fury that the woman got out of bed and followed her. She found Jose, unconscious but thrashing under the covers, his eyes rolled back into his head. At the hospital, doctors diagnosed bacterial meningitis. If Brat hadn't made such a commotion, Jose might not have gotten help in time to avoid brain damage—or death.

Dogs have also been known to get upset and go for help when someone is incapacitated. I read accounts of people being alerted by their dogs to a grandmother, lying on the floor after a stroke; to a man, thrown off his tractor, his ribs and pelvis crushed; and to people hemorrhaging, having seizures, and suffering from insulin shock. Once a man caught his arm in a snow blower and slumped, bleeding, in the driveway. His dog came to the rescue by going to find the man's wife.

———

THEN THERE was Girl.

When lightning struck several trees on Ray Ellis's twenty acres in Martins Ferry, Ohio, he took his German shepherd, named Girl, with him to cut the trees for firewood. As always, Girl sat beside him and guarded him like a sentinel. Even the chain saw's roar in her sensitive ears could not make her leave Ray.

He had found her, lost and bedraggled, at his mail box a few years earlier and had brought her home. After two months of searching for her owners, Ray had given up.

"She's mine," Ray had told his wife, Dorothy. "We're going to keep her."

Girl became fiercely loyal to him, perhaps in gratitude.

While Ray sawed one tree into logs, loaded the wood on a tractor, and took it home, Girl stayed with him. They returned for a second tree that had crashed down on a sapling and pressed it to the ground. As Ray sawed the tree into pieces, the sapling sprang up, hit him in the head, and knocked him out. The chain saw, still running, cut his groin in five places and sliced his ankle to the bone.

Girl bent over Ray, lying in a pool of blood. She sniffed him, whimpered, and seemed to understand his danger. As the saw cut into the ground and finally stopped, Girl shot back to the house for help. Dorothy noticed her from the window but assumed only that Ray was on his way home since the dog never left him for an instant.

But Ray never arrived. Girl continued to bark frantically outside. When Dorothy did not respond, the German shepherd threw herself at the front door until Dorothy opened it. Girl barked with even greater urgency and ran to a corner of the yard near the woods, then back to the house.

"What are you trying to tell me?" Dorothy asked.

Girl "answered" in the only way she could: She barked and ran toward the woods again.

Following her, Dorothy found Ray lying on the ground next to his chain saw. He must have turned it off and decided to take a nap, she figured. She'd misunderstood Girl; the dog had only been playing, not trying to make Dorothy follow her.

"Dinner's ready," Dorothy called. "Come on. Let's go home."

Ray did not move.

As she stepped closer, Dorothy saw the blood splattered all around Ray's body. Breathless from fear, she dashed back to the house and called an ambulance.

Girl, still huddled beside Ray, tried to fight off the medics who returned with Dorothy. Only when Dorothy grasped the German shepherd's collar and held her back did the dog stop protecting Ray and let the medics approach. And while Ray recovered in the hospital, Girl refused to eat and pined for him at home. Even in his absence, she was loyal.

———

DOGS CAN do more than merely bark and run to get help for sick or injured people. When Judi Bayly's oxygen mask slipped off in the middle of the night, an alarm sounded. Her Irish setter Lyric tried to rouse her but could not. The dog knocked the receiver off a telephone and pressed a preprogrammed, speed-dial button three times to call 911.

An act of compassion? Probably, but no one can be certain because Lyric was a service dog, carefully trained to call for help over the phone in just that way.

However, in a true story from *Pet Heroes* by Paul Simons, Gemma, an ordinary mutt, had absolutely no training and acted straight from the heart to take care of Darren Mahon. After he had a seizure and fell, unconscious, to the floor in Birmingham, England, Gemma waited until the telephone rang, pushed the receiver off its hook, and yapped like crazy. Worried that the yaps meant Mahon was in trouble, the caller came to the house, found Mahon lying there, and called an ambulance.

IF ANIMALS are unable to find help for the person in a medical crisis, they sometimes attempt to help the person themselves. In many instances these creatures have shown great compassion and an uncanny sense about what was needed by the person in trouble.

• Trixie, a mixed-breed dog, was alone in the house with Jack Fyfe when he had a stroke in Sydney, Australia. Paralyzed and unable to leave his bed, Fyfe had no way of getting water to drink—so he asked Trixie to bring him water. She went to the bathroom, picked up a towel in her teeth, soaked it in her water bowl, and dragged the towel back to Fyfe. Trixie then draped it over his face, so he could suck the water from it.

When she'd used up all the water in her bowl, she wet the towel in the toilet and brought it to Fyfe. For nine days—until his family noticed his absence at a party and came to check on him—Trixie kept him from dying of dehydration. Fyfe went to the hospital for five months of rehabilitation, and then came home again to her.

• Scout, a Labrador retriever in Waurika, Oklahoma, wagged his tail eagerly when eighty-four-year-old Mary Gladys Baker came outside to check on him one cold night. Dressed in just a nightgown and a light coat, she slipped, fell, and broke her hip. She lay helpless on the ground and shivered from cold and pain. Recognizing her distress, Scout went back to his dog house, grabbed his old quilt in his teeth, and dragged it to her. He covered her with the quilt, then lay down beside her and kept her warm until help arrived the next morning.

• Bug, an Oklahoma cat whose story was told in *Cat Fancy* magazine, watched her owner cough and sneeze in bed with a 102-degree fever. The woman had nothing in the house to relieve her symptoms because her son had used all the flu medicine the week before. Dejected and miserable, she cried until she fell asleep. When she woke, Bug was sitting on her bed next to a little pile of get-well surprises that he'd gathered together and set on her blanket: a cat toy, an earring she'd lost, and a dirty foil package that Bug had probably batted out from under a bed. In the package was a nasty, dusty throat lozenge.

WHEN ROZ BROWN'S daughter brought home treats for Holly, a West Highland terrier in Cambridge, England, the dog was ecstatic. The tempting little morsels were called jelly babies, an English version of gummy bears that are shaped like infants and rolled in granulated sugar.

Holly squeaked and jumped up on her hind legs at her first sniff of candy. When she was given two jelly babies, she gulped them down, then smacked her lips and wagged her tail to ask for more. But two were enough, Brown decided. Her daughter laid the bag on the sitting room table.

Not long after her daughter left, Brown, a diabetic for thirty-eight years, began to feel weak and sick. Her blood-sugar level dropped so low that she fell, unconscious, to the floor. Holly seemed to realize that Brown needed help; she scrambled over to the jelly babies and nosed the bag off the table to the rug. Even though she'd been desperate for the candy just minutes earlier, she did not gobble it down. Instead, she nudged two jelly babies out of the bag and across the room—and left them beside Brown's mouth. Then Holly nuzzled the woman to rouse her.

When Brown's eyes fluttered open, Holly was sitting patiently beside her with two jelly babies. Brown had just enough strength to put them into her mouth; they gave her the energy she needed to reach for the other two candies in the bag. After she ate them, she managed to get to the kitchen for more substantial food, which raised her blood sugar back up to a safe level.

"TINA IS the dog from hell," Nora Martyniak of Lakeville, Massachusetts, complained to her friend Susan.

As they worked on Nora's income tax form, Tina, an energetic black mongrel, pranced into Nora's living room with the speed of lightning. She paced, circled the rug, sniffed, whined, yipped, and refused to lie down and be quiet. Since she'd been adopted into her new home two weeks earlier, "nervous" and "peripatetic" had become her personal adjectives.

Tina's life, before coming to the Martyniak's, had not been easy. Her previous family had rescued her, a ragamuffin, from the pound just hours before she was to be destroyed. They tried to adjust to Tina's energy, but in a few short months, her unruly behavior had worn them down, and they decided to get rid of her. When they asked Nora if she would take Tina, Nora felt sorry for her, about to be dumped a second time.

But, her husband, Steve, was adamant: "No dog!"

It took a fight to change his mind.

Grudgingly, he went to pick up Tina. Once he was stuck with her, he tried to make the best of the nerve-assaulting situation. Steve gave Tina cookies, played games with her, and took her for runs in the snow to curb her ceaseless energy. He quickly became her best friend, but her devotion to him could not lessen the daily stress of living with her insecurity and constant wiggling. Tina was a difficult dog to appreciate.

Now she yapped near the sofa while Nora and Susan worked on the income taxes. When Steve walked through the living room after shoveling snow, Tina darted over and greeted him with joy.

"Keep her here for a while, will you?" Steve asked Nora. "I'm going to read the paper. I need some peace and quiet."

Steve went into the den, lay down on his brown tweed recliner, and glanced at the headlines. Nora held onto Tina to prevent her from pestering him. But the dog was being a nuisance: She panted, yipped, and refused to give up hope of joining Steve.

Suddenly, her eagerness changed to alarm. She jumped up and pricked her ears. Her fur stood on end. She planted her paws firmly on Nora's knee, barked, and leaped on her lap.

"Be quiet!" Nora warned, not understanding Tina's urgency. Nora turned to Susan. "Tina's going into her dog-from-hell mode again."

As Nora held the dog's collar to keep her from lunging at Susan, Tina tugged so violently, trying to escape, that she almost broke Nora's fingers.

"All right! All right!" Nora released her.

Tina raced into the den, then ran back into the living room, barked and yapped insistently, ran back to Steve, and then to Nora and Susan—again and again. Each time Tina tore into the den, she jumped on Steve's recliner and made it rock and squeak under her weight.

Nora's patience grew as thin as tissue paper. "She's usually not this bad. I can't imagine what they're doing."

When Susan left a few minutes later, Nora went into the den to find out for herself. Everything seemed normal—Steve was lying on the recliner, resting, his hands on his chest, exactly as he always did while taking naps. But Tina was jumping up and down on his chest and pushing her nose into his mouth to open it. Each time it snapped shut, she pushed it open again.

This game is ridiculous, Nora thought. "How can you sleep with that crazy dog all over you?"

There was no response from Steve.

Nora walked toward him. She intended to disengage Tina and let Steve take his nap in peace. In horror, she realized that his face was blue. She pulled Tina away, but the dog fought her and kept trying to force Steve's mouth open to help him breathe.

Nora, terrified, was scarcely breathing herself. She dragged Tina to the kitchen, called the police, and ran back to Steve, whose face had turned more blue than ever. While Tina barked furiously behind the kitchen door, Nora tried the only CPR she knew: She beat Steve's chest, opened his mouth, and breathed into it. But she was no more successful than Tina had been at keeping Steve's lips open; his mouth kept closing because he was lying down.

When the police and paramedics arrived, they administered oxygen and managed to resuscitate Steve. They brought him to the hospital for tests and observations, but, mysteriously, an EKG revealed no evidence of a heart attack. Doctors were never certain why he'd stopped breathing.

One thing was certain, however: Tina had known that Steve was in trouble even at a distance, when she was in the living room, unable to see him in the den. Once Tina had reached him, she'd also tried to help him breathe, just as Nora had, with CPR.

After that day, Nora changed her opinion of Tina. She was no dog from hell. She was an angel.

CHAPTER FOUR

SELFLESS GUARDIANS

WHEN A three-year-old boy fell into the gorilla compound at a Brookfield, Illinois, zoo, Binti Jua, a 150-pound female lowland gorilla, cradled and stroked him, then carried him to a door, where zoo staff members reached in and took him to the hospital. Binti's behavior surprised many people at the time because they thought that no gorilla—or any other animal—could be so compassionate.

Ten years earlier, however, Jambo, a male silverback gorilla at the Jersey Wildlife Preservation Trust in England, had extended himself even more to be kind to Levan Merriott, age five, in a similar crisis. The little boy had climbed onto a wall surrounding the gorillas' enclosure, lost his balance, and fallen twenty feet to a concrete water drain. Jambo found him, unconscious, with blood trickling from his nose and mouth.

The gorilla would not let his three wives and offspring, who shared the compound, come near Levan. If they approached, Jambo stuck out his arm and shoved them back. He sat down by Levan, sniffed him all over, and gently caressed him. When Levan regained consciousness and started to cry, Jambo got upset himself. He ushered his family away and held them back from Levan until a zoo official climbed the wall and carried him out of the enclosure.

Not only gorillas, but many other captive and domestic animals have made just as much effort as Jambo did to protect people from other animals who might harm them.

In another true story related in *Pet Heroes* by Paul Simons, Bruno Cipriano was chopping wood in Italy, and his docile cow Carletta was grazing nearby. Without warning, a wild boar charged, gored Bruno, and knocked him to the ground. Before the boar could finish him off, Carletta lowered her horns and attacked the boar. She butted him even as he fled, then stood by to protect Cipriano until his wife brought help.

MIKE AND JILL Evans were not sure whether they should buy Smokey, a buckskin horse, for their son, Justin. Smokey had not been gelded until age fourteen; perhaps his many years as a stud might have made him aggressive. He'd also been a polo pony and could run like the wind, much too fast for a five-year-old child.

In spite of these potential problems, Jill wanted to try out the horse. As she and Justin rode him through a field on their ranch in Piedmont, Oklahoma, he accidentally startled a wild turkey. It flapped its wings and flew between Smokey's legs and into his face. Though most horses would have gotten spooked and thrown their riders, Smokey was calm. He kept on going without a flinch.

"Protecting Justin was the most important thing to him," Jill told Mike.

Relieved to have found a horse they could trust with their child, they bought Smokey.

In the next two years Justin and Smokey won many ribbons in barrel-racing and pole-bending competitions. The boy and his horse were inseparable. Whenever Justin called Smokey in the pasture, the horse ran eagerly to him.

"Smokey is my best friend," Justin told everyone.

Justin was thrilled to be riding his best friend in a cattle drive down Agnew Street in Oklahoma City one afternoon. He and his parents and a few other riders led the drive out of the stockyard; over two hundred more riders followed the herd. The crowd stood behind cars parked along the street; hundreds of people watched, clapped, and cheered. Smokey, imperturbable, ignored the noise and clopped along on steady hooves.

The longhorns, however, were not so even-tempered. All the riders' jostling and shoving from behind had made the cattle nervous. As they rounded the corner just out of the stockyard, they stampeded. Crashing into parked cars, they lunged onto the sidewalks as people ran for their lives.

Mike, Jill, and Justin heard hooves thundering behind them and tried to get out of the way. As they maneuvered their horses toward the curb, Justin somehow got separated from his parents. Even worse, the parked cars blocked him and Smokey from getting to safety. As the longhorns rumbled closer, the boy and his horse were trapped directly in the herd's path.

Justin yelled for help. His parents froze, powerless to help him. Then, to slow down the herd and give Justin more time to escape, Jill and another rider turned their horses toward each other and blocked part of the street. But a steer charged between them, pushed them apart, and led the way for the rest of the herd. In seconds, a sea of cattle engulfed Justin and Smokey. The air filled with the sound of longhorns snorting, hooves pounding, and rock-solid bodies thudding against each other.

Certain that she was about to see her son be trampled to death, Jill held her breath. There was nothing she could do to save him. In order to protect himself, Smokey would rear back and kick the longhorns, as any horse would do. Justin would be thrown off his saddle. The cattle's hooves would quickly grind his bones into the pavement.

But Jill had underestimated Smokey. As the longhorns bumped and jostled him, he did *not* fight back. Just as he'd remained calm when the wild turkey flew in his face, Smokey stood his ground.

A steer rammed into Smokey and Justin, then tried to shove his way around them. The steer slipped and fell, slamming his huge body into Smokey's hindquarters. To avoid being knocked down, Smokey lifted a leg and let the steer slide under him. But the longhorn, instead of sliding through and moving on, shoved his body under Smokey's belly, stood up, and raised the horse and Justin into the air.

Justin was so far off the pavement, being on top of both Smokey *and* the steer, that all he could do was scream and kick and try to save himself. Yet once more Smokey stayed calm. Without resisting, the horse rested on the steer, who was scrambling to regain his balance. But the longhorn staggered and again crashed to the pavement.

Smokey did not go down with him. Still composed, the horse raised his back leg, stepped over the steer's body, and kept moving. Slowly Smokey worked his way through the herd to the side of the street. There he stopped and waited, with Justin safe on his back, while the longhorns passed.

After Smokey had protected him in such a crisis, Justin realized, more than ever, that the horse truly *was* his best friend.

IN ORDER to protect the people they care about, cats and dogs have even faced down animals much bigger and more powerful than they are. Kelli Kinsman of Dracut, Massachusetts, wrote to *Cat Fancy* magazine about Flash, her delicate eight-and-a-half-pound part-Siamese, who threw herself at a huge dog that was attacking Kinsman. Flash wrapped herself around his throat and clawed his eyes. The dog ran away, defeated.

Grizzly Bear, a hefty 180-pound St. Bernard, was just as courageous. One day Mrs. David Gratias heard a suspicious noise behind her cabin in Denali, Alaska, and, curious, went out with her dog to investigate. She left her front door ajar, so she could listen for her infant daughter Theresa, who lay asleep in her crib.

When Gratias discovered a young grizzly cub in the backyard, she had an alarming thought: Surely its mother had already gone through the open front door and attacked Theresa! Tearing back to her baby, she turned the corner of the cabin and ran straight into the eight-foot mother bear. The startled bear reared on her hind legs, roared, and hovered over Gratias like a giant in a nightmare.

The bear slashed at her with massive paws, and Gratias shrank back to protect herself. But she was even more desperate to protect Theresa. Instead of running to safety, Gratias tried to get past the bear to the front door, but she slipped and fell at the grizzly's feet. The bear stooped down, raked her sharp claws across the woman's cheek, and sank them into her shoulder.

The grizzly bared her teeth, about to bite into Gratias, when her dog sprang to her defense. Seemingly fearless about challenging such a huge animal, the dog attacked, barking, snapping, and lunging at the bear. As the St. Bernard shielded Gratias with his body, she fainted.

When she opened her eyes, her dog had turned from a vicious protector to a compassionate nurse; he was gently licking her face and trying to revive her. She thought instantly of Theresa. Certain that the mother bear had killed her child, Gratias forced herself to stand and staggered into the cabin. Fortunately, Theresa was still safely asleep.

The St. Bernard had fought so nimbly that he had no wounds. Though he was splattered with blood, it belonged to the bear and Gratias, whose wounds slowly healed.

———

DEBBIE INIONS rode out early one evening on her quarter horse, Pat, to check the cattle on her farm in Alberta, Canada. As the sky darkened over the farm's 2,100 acres, she took a shortcut through some brush. Hustler, her German shepherd, bounded through the grass beside her.

As they headed up a hill, a sudden rustling in the bushes startled Pat. He shied, jumped, and brushed against a fence. Since he couldn't run through it, he whirled around and shied again. Debbie, thrown off-balance, fell to the ground. Her leg was shattered. Blood poured from the wound where a broken bone had torn through her skin.

She lay crumpled on the steep hill. Everything seemed blurred; overwhelming pain throbbed through her body. Hustler rushed over and sniffed her as if he wanted to help, but she needed more than he could offer. She needed a doctor as quickly as she could get to one.

But no one would find her, she feared, for many hours. Her children were home, asleep, and would not miss her. Her husband, Brian, was out seeding barley; he probably wouldn't come home and see that she was gone until well after midnight. Even when he *did* begin searching, it might be morning by the time he found her.

Why would he even think of looking in the middle of the brush a quarter of a mile from the nearest road?

With Hustler beside her, Debbie tried to push her pain to the back of her mind, so she could concentrate on what to do. Maybe if she could get Pat to go home, someone would see him walking along with an empty saddle and know that she was in trouble. But when she swished a stick at him, he took off through the bush, in a direction where no one would ever see him.

Crestfallen, Debbie told herself that she'd have to get up and walk home on her own, no matter how bad the pain was. But each time she tried to move, her broken bones scraped together, causing more waves of excruciating pain. After she tried to stand three times, the agony was so overwhelming that she thought she'd faint. Exhausted, she lay down beside Hustler. He moved closer, and his furry body kept her warm.

Hustler had proved to be an exceptional dog, a rare combination of aggression and sensitivity. With the energy of three ranch hands, he herded cattle. He nipped at their legs to keep them moving and loaded them onto chutes. But he was also extremely gentle. Hustler's breeder had told Debbie that the dog had once picked up a baby bird who had fallen from its nest. Hustler carried the bird in his mouth to the breeder and had seemed concerned about the tiny fledgling.

Knowing Hustler's capacity for compassion, Debbie was shocked when he abruptly pricked his ears, stood up, and shot down the hill. How could he be so *unconcerned* about her? How could he possibly amuse himself chasing deer when she was so badly hurt? Especially when, at any moment, she might go into shock or bleed to death?

He returned, stood over her, bared his teeth, and growled into the darkness. She'd never seen him look so fierce. Squinting to figure out just what he was growling at, Debbie saw two coyotes only fifteen feet away. They curled their lips and growled back at Hustler. Creeping closer, their paws crunched on leaves and underbrush.

Debbie cringed, the back of her neck prickling with terror. Coyotes rarely approached a person unless they felt threatened. Perhaps she was close to their den and was upsetting them. Whatever their problem, these two could easily attack her, she believed. For protection, she leaned closer to Hustler. He snarled, leaped over her, and chased the coyotes back into the brush again.

Debbie heard thrashing, barking, angry snapping, and pained yipping. The darkness and thick brush prevented her from seeing who was winning the fight. She lay there, faint and queasy, not knowing whether Hustler or the coyotes would emerge from the brush.

When Hustler finally returned, Debbie was immensely grateful. Once again, the dog switched from fierce aggression to pure kindness. He lay down beside her, apparently trying to warm her, and gently licked and cleaned her bloody leg.

Every few minutes, throughout the night, the coyotes would circle around her. She kept screaming at them to scare them off, and each time Hustler chased them back into the bush. Debbie listened to the snarling and the snapping of every encounter. Gripped by fear, she waited to see whether Hustler would win. Each time he returned. But the odds were against him, two to one, and she wasn't sure how long he could last, no matter how much he wanted to protect her.

The coyotes howled, and rain started to fall. The wind picked up. Debbie began trembling so violently from cold and shock that the shaking hurt her leg. She was afraid she'd pass out from the pain.

"Get a grip, Deb," she kept repeating.

She had to stay conscious in order to defend herself. And Hustler also had to stay alert. She hung on to him, *willing* him not to relax his vigil. He pressed against her as if to reassure her that he was there.

About 1:30 that morning, Brian came home from the barley fields and found all the windows open. He was immediately concerned: Debbie always closed them in the evening. When he also discovered that her horse and riding boots were missing, his concern escalated to anxiety. He rushed to his daughter's room and shook her awake.

"Where's your mother?"

"She went to check the cows."

Brian told himself not to worry; he would find her. Yet his body tensed as he ran to his all-terrain vehicle and started combing the farm for Debbie. About 4 A.M., Brian caught sight of Hustler in the car's headlights. The German shepherd was chasing two coyotes through a clearing. Debbie had to be close by.

Brian turned off the motor and ran after Hustler. "Debbie? Debbie!" he called through the wind.

She heard him but was so weak and hoarse that she could barely whisper. Straining to listen, Brian finally heard her answer. Then Hustler appeared and led Brian to her.

"Thank God, you found me!" Debbie moaned.

Her pain was so intense that Brian dared not try to move her. He would have to go for help. As he sped away, Debbie looked around, afraid again. Where was Hustler? The dog was gone. Perhaps he'd followed Brian home and left her all alone.

But she never should have doubted his devotion to her. When the coyotes resumed their howling in the brush, Hustler returned and crouched beside her head. Each time the coyotes drew close, he chased them off, as he'd managed to do for nearly seven hours. After each fight, he curled up protectively beside her.

Brian left a flashing light on the road to signal the paramedics and rushed back to Debbie with blankets. Just before dawn, the ambulance arrived. Paramedics loaded Debbie onto a stretcher, then into the ambulance. The coyotes watched, panting, from less than forty feet away.

For the next two weeks, Debbie recuperated in the hospital. Hustler waited at home and refused to eat. Whenever Brian returned from visiting her, Hustler raced to the truck and peered inside. Each time he saw that she wasn't there, his eyes looked sad and troubled.

Debbie finally did come home. She opened the truck door; and before she could climb out, Hustler, ecstatic, jumped up to rest his feet on the running board. He seemed to sense how fragile she was, and instead of pushing against her for affection, he carefully sniffed her broken leg from toe to hip.

Through four surgeries the following year, Debbie slowly graduated from a wheelchair to a walker to crutches to a cane. No matter what method she used to get around, Hustler followed her every move and guarded her. When Debbie was finally well enough to ride Pat again to check the cattle, Hustler was her ever-present guard, a graceful silhouette crossing the fields in the moonlight.

———

LATE ONE dismal January afternoon, Chester Jenkins went out to break the ice in a water trough on his forty-acre farm near Springfield, Missouri. He was a strong, stocky man, used to bad weather and hard work. Still, just four months earlier he'd had heart-bypass surgery. Though he felt well enough, he was still vulnerable.

As he walked toward the cattle pen, his two-year-old chocolate Labrador–Chesapeake Bay retriever, Bailey, trotted along behind. The dog, rescued as a pup from the Humane Society, had been a Christmas gift to Jenkins's son. When the boy left for college, Bailey had transferred his loyalty to Jenkins.

The dog followed him around from morning till night and always tried to help with chores or anything else that Jenkins was doing. If he patted a mare, Bailey jumped up and licked her to add his share of affection. When Jenkins herded cattle, Bailey became such an ardent shepherd that Jenkins had to lock him up till the work was done.

As Jenkins tossed ice to the ground and refilled the tank with water, Bailey sat outside the pen and waited to escort him home. Jenkins poured feed into another trough, then opened the gate to let in his cows and the two-thousand-pound Belgian Blue bull he'd recently leased.

The cows were docile, but the bull was not. All muscle and strength, he'd been injured years ago and still seemed resentful about it. Or, at least, that was Jenkins's explanation for why the bull behaved like someone spoiling for a fight. When people approached, he stamped his hooves, snorted, and bellowed so vehemently that the ground almost shook. He seemed to carry truck-sized grudges and had a worse temper than any of the other bulls.

As the cattle started eating, Jenkins picked up his buckets and turned to the gate. Suddenly, he felt something bump his hip and knew he was in trouble. The Belgian Blue was after him. Jenkins tried to run, but the bull was too fast. The bull lowered his head, snapped it under Jenkins's body, and flipped him twenty feet through the air.

Jenkins landed in a metal water tank and rammed his shoulder so hard that the metal bent. He bounced off the side, back into the bull's path. As Jenkins lay in the mud, practically under the bull's hooves, the animal loomed over him. Defenseless and racked with pain, Jenkins curled up to protect himself.

The bull bellowed and began to trample him. Again and again the animal scraped his hooves down Jenkins's back. Then the bull seemed to change his mind and consider another method of attack. He backed off and prepared to charge.

Jenkins's mind raced with desperate thoughts of how to escape. But he was helpless. If he were flipped back into the air, his heart-bypass incision would surely rip open, and then the bull would stamp him to a bloody pulp.

Jenkins was certain he was going to die, yet he kept asking himself, "What can I do? What can I do?" The terrifying answer was "Nothing."

Then he saw a streak of fur the color of Bailey's Irish Cream. Growling and snapping, his dog crawled under the fence, leaped over Jenkins, and charged the bull. Bailey sank his teeth deep into the animal's face and refused to loosen his jaws no matter how hard the bull shook him. The bull tossed his head and slammed Bailey to the ground. Again the dog sprang up, bit the bull's nose, and stubbornly hung on. The bull shook his head so violently that he threw Bailey across the pen. The dog barked and snarled and attacked again until the bull turned away—and Jenkins rolled under the fence to safety.

Bailey ran back and sniffed Jenkins as if he were trying to see how badly he was hurt. Jenkins didn't think he'd ever be able to stand again—his shoulder, ribs, and hip throbbed unbearably. But evening was coming; the temperature would soon drop below zero. He couldn't lie there in the ice and mud and freeze to death.

Jenkins tried to clear his mind and figure out what to do. "Go find Mom," he moaned.

Bailey dashed to the house.

After Jenkins gathered his strength, he managed to sit, then stand. But he could hardly breathe, and his body ached so much that he was sure he could not walk.

"Your legs are fine," he reminded himself. "You can make it home." He staggered toward the lighted windows of his house.

There he found Bailey trying to get the attention of Jenkins's wife, Iris Ann, by whimpering and clawing at the front door. Although the dog was never permitted inside the house, he seemed to realize that Jenkins's injury allowed for an exception. After Jenkins opened the door, Bailey helped him steady himself and stagger into the kitchen. The minute Iris Ann laid eyes on her husband, she rushed to hold him up before he collapsed.

"I need a doctor," Jenkins said, barely able to speak.

Iris Ann called an ambulance while Jenkins—afraid that if he lay on the sofa, he'd never get up—sank down on a stool. Bailey pressed himself against Jenkins's leg and refused to move until the fire chief arrived and Iris Ann ordered Bailey out.

Still, the dog seemed to feel that his rescue was not finished. He planted himself in front of the house, watched the road with intense eyes, and waited for the ambulance. When the paramedics finally came, he barked and whined and ran in circles as if he were trying to tell the men to hurry. Then he herded them into the kitchen as quickly as he could make them run.

Jenkins spent eleven days in the hospital. All of his ribs were crushed on one side, one shoulder blade was fractured, a lung was punctured, and his hip was severely bruised. Luckily, the stitches from his bypass operation had not ripped open. In fact, if he hadn't had that surgery before his trauma with the bull, the doctors said, the shock would have killed him.

When Jenkins got home, he thanked his dog. Though he was normally a crusty, unsentimental man, Jenkins rewarded Bailey with a feast of ham and cookies, and the family talked of buying him a special dog house with air-conditioning. They said that Bailey had been as heroic as Lassie.

Bailey didn't seem to notice the fuss. He only seemed to care that Jenkins was home, safe. Bailey was content to resume his normal routine of waiting outside in the snow for him. And when Jenkins appeared, Bailey continued to follow him like a shadow and help him with his daily chores.

CHAPTER FIVE

NATURAL CARETAKERS

A NIMALS SEEM to know when a person needs to be comforted. In fact, a marriage-and-family counselor once told me that he always watches where his clients' dogs sit during therapy; whoever they choose to be near, the counselor believes, is the family member suffering the most emotional pain.

In *Guideposts,* Penny Silvius Gillett, also a counselor, describes her golden retriever, Francine, who was so sensitive to clients' feelings that she became a therapist herself. Francine once got up from her spot under Gillett's desk and padded across the office to curl up at the feet of a man who was so shy and reserved that he could barely talk. By her mere presence, the dog relaxed him enough that his words began to flow freely, greatly aiding the therapeutic process. Another time, Francine, seeking affection, put her paws in the lap of a woman who was bitter and withdrawn. The woman's face softened into smiles at the dog—whose compassion became a turning point in the therapy, Gillett believes, as well as in the woman's life.

Francine seemed to know exactly whom to console and how best to do the consoling. When clients were anxious, lonely, or angry, Francine rested her chin on their laps and looked up at them with brown eyes full of understanding. Sensing a person's distress brought her, full of heart, to help.

Other animals have tried just as hard to show concern for emotionally troubled people.

"WE ARE *not* going to get a dog," Kermit Essex told his wife, Cheryl.

She refused to listen. When an ad for a litter of mutts appeared in their town newspaper in Garden City, South Carolina, Cheryl insisted that he at least go with her to *look* at them.

Five fat puppies waddled into the room. Delighted, Cheryl bent down to play with them.

"We're *not* getting a dog," Kermit reminded her.

The runt of the litter, a skinny, silver mixture of schnauzer and West Highland terrier, shyly joined her siblings. Kermit picked her up, and she licked his face.

"We're taking this one," he said. "Let's go. Right now."

Kermit and Cheryl named the runt Rosie O'Grady, after a bar in New York. Rosie grew up to be a respectable twenty-five pounds, not bad for a runt. She also became totally loyal to Kermit, the very person who had not wanted a dog. At night Rosie cuddled under his arm on one side of the bed, Kermit slept in the middle, and Cheryl was crowded into what little remained of the other edge.

This sleeping arrangement only changed when Kermit traveled out of town for his consulting business. Before he left on each trip, he always told Rosie, "Take care of Mama."

And she did.

But when Kermit was gone, the dog wouldn't sleep in the bed no matter how much Cheryl tried to coax her. Instead, Rosie slept alone on the porch sofa and pined for him.

On one of Kermit's trips out of town, pining inexplicably turned to sudden viciousness. She growled, barked, and tried to bite Cheryl, who was stunned at the aggression.

An hour later, a telephone call accounted for Rosie's strange behavior: "Your husband has been killed in a plane crash."

Cheryl believes that Rosie had already "known."

Grief stricken, Cheryl went to bed that night and cried. Rosie, who had never once been in bed with her when Kermit traveled, seemed to understand that Cheryl needed help. The dog left her hand-crocheted afghan on the porch sofa, trotted across the house, and curled up next to Cheryl on the bed. Since Kermit's death, the little mutt has slept beside her as protector and comforter.

More than Kermit ever would have predicted, Rosie had been "taking care of Mama."

———

THE MUTT had many breeds in his genetic code: German shepherd, greyhound, golden and Labrador retrievers. Abandoned in front of a New York City police station, he was picked up by a woman who was not allowed to have dogs in her apartment. To save him from certain death at the pound, she passed him to friends for a few nights at a time, along what they called a canine "underground railroad."

One stop along the "railroad" was the apartment of Shirley Guy, an actress and playwright who also happened to be clinically depressed. Unable to work for five years, she'd been sitting at home, brooding, and mourning the deaths of her mother, her best friend, and her dog.

"Get another dog," Guy's therapist urged.

"I can't deal with another one," Guy insisted, even after she'd fallen in love with the mutt when it made a stop at her "station" along the "railroad."

After two nights, she hardened her heart and sent him on his way. When he was offered a permanent home as a guard in a Bronx liquor store, however, something snapped in her.

"He's too sweet to be a guard dog," Guy said. "I'm going to get him back. I'm keeping him. He's mine."

Guy named the mongrel Dylan, after the poet Dylan Thomas, and took him back to her apartment, where she was also keeping Frisky, a friend's cocker spaniel, overnight. When Guy gave Dylan a dog biscuit, Frisky stole it. Then he whined because it was too big for him to chew. Dylan graciously took the milkbone back, cracked it in half, crumbled one of the halves, and left the small pieces in a pile for Frisky. Astonished by his generosity, Guy had no doubt that keeping him had been right.

Dylan was gentle and attentive. As time went on, he seemed to take upon himself consoling Guy and bringing her out of her depression. When he wanted more dinner, he carried his empty food bowl in his teeth to the living room; his clowning made her laugh for the first time in years. On their walks in the park, he sailed over benches with the grace of Rudolf Nureyev, then stopped, turned around, and looked at Guy to check her reaction.

Guy felt certain that Dylan *wanted* her to be happy. On bleak days when she really didn't feel like smiling, she made herself smile for *his* sake. She wanted to show him that he'd been successful in cheering her up, as he was so obviously trying to do. After a few months, she realized that she didn't have to force herself to smile anymore; she felt like smiling. Soon, she was even laughing with all the new friends she made on walks with Dylan in the park.

If Guy felt anxious on the walks, Dylan understood and leaned protectively against her legs to calm her. Or he looked up at her with expressive eyes that made her feel safe and cherished.

"That dog radiates love," passersby told her on the street.

Supported by that love, Guy took a computer class and started writing again. Two years after the mutt had come to live with her, one of her plays was produced by La Mama Experimental Theater Club in New York. When the play closed, Guy began writing a book and traveling with Dylan to writer's conferences.

"When he's with me, I feel I can do anything," she told her friends. "Whatever I try to do will work out just fine."

With Dylan, her attitude had drastically changed from brooding and depression.

MEDUSA, the dog of veterinarian Mark Esser, had an ominous name that evoked images of snakes for hair. She was also a Doberman pinscher, a breed that can terrify people. When visitors came to Esser's home in Sewell, New Jersey, they were often frightened when they heard her bark, and they froze, thinking that she would lunge at them through the front window.

When a new neighbor moved in across the street, Medusa trotted amiably over to meet him. She wagged her stump of a tail, panted a friendly welcome, and waited expectantly to be welcomed back.

"She's giving me the evil eye!" the neighbor shouted. "Is she going to bite?"

She'd only hoped that he would play with her, just as she played with the neighborhood children, Esser explained to the man. Every time she saw any of the children, she sniffed and nuzzled them. All she wanted was people's petting and affection.

Medusa was so loving that Esser sent her, like a roving therapist, to comfort people in distress.

One of them was a client, still distraught and crying all the time weeks after her dog had died from bone cancer. Daily, she carried her dog's ashes to her mailbox, so that he could "accompany" her as he'd done for many years. She refused to get another dog to ease her sadness. It could die, too, she insisted to Esser. She could never face such sorrow twice.

The woman needed grief counseling, but she was not likely to seek it out, and Esser, no psychologist himself, felt unqualified to help her. But Medusa could do it, he decided. Her sensitivity, which seemed to come so naturally, would have great healing power.

"Would you like for Medusa to visit you?" Esser asked the woman.

"All right," she agreed, but hesitantly.

Medusa bounded into her house as if she owned it. She plastered herself against the woman, who buried her face in Medusa's fur and cried. The dog, sensing that she was supposed to bring solace, stood, still and silent, beside the woman and let her pour out her sadness. Then Medusa nudged the woman's hand to ask for pets.

Medusa visited regularly for several months. Her comfort-dog therapy worked.

"Medusa got me through the roughest of times," the woman told Esser.

Her use of the past tense "got" showed that she had been healed.

Medusa also went to live with a man who was dying of lung cancer during his last month. She sat beside him and refused to leave except to eat or take a brief respite outdoors. When he grew too weak to get up from his chair, Medusa lay her head in his lap *for hours.* Finally, he had to go to the hospital, but Medusa stayed on to soothe his wife. Whenever she came home, sad from visiting her husband, Medusa was waiting for her with sympathetic whimpers.

No matter who needed comfort, Medusa, the "savage" Doberman, was there for them.

CATS CAN be exceptionally sensitive to someone in emotional turmoil. In their own way, they can soothe and calm people with as much compassion as dogs.

Sambal, a New York City Siamese, was named for an Indonesian spice. She showed natural mediation skills during the squabbles of Janice Hopkins Tanne and her husband. When their discussions heated up to tiffs, Sambal, looking upset, sat between the couple, meowed, and forced them to pay attention to her until they cooled off again.

Letters to *Cat Fancy* magazine describe other cats who have comforted people who were upset or troubled.

• Felipe, a Siamese, jumped onto the lap of a woman who was crying about her husband's upcoming back surgery. The cat looked at her with eyes that seemed full of concern. He licked her cheeks and raised his paw to her face as if he were petting her. His compassion made her less worried and afraid.

• Peaches helped her companion, who often suffered from nightmares. The cat would get up from her usual sleeping spot at the woman's ankles, go to her pillow, and paw her face. Then Peaches would purr until the woman opened her eyes, a signal to the cat that the bad dream was over. After that, she would go back to her place at the woman's feet.

• Porkchop, a portly male tabby, hung around a law school seemingly wanting to comfort jittery students. One of them was a woman who was anxious about her bar exam, which would take place in a few days. As she packed to go to the hotel where she would stay while taking the test, Porkchop followed her from her dorm room to her car. He seemed intent on visiting with her. Even though she wanted to hurry to the hotel and study, she sat on the grass with him, petted him, and told him about her loneliness and fear. Porkchop's attentiveness made the woman feel that he understood her distress. Later, she passed the exam.

———

BEFORE THEIR marriage, Georgene and Jim Lockwood of Prescott, Arizona, both felt that they had cats who offered extraordinary comfort in emotional crises.

• Georgene's pet was Duffy, an orange tiger cat whose veterinarian named him "The Terror." The entire clinic staff had to hold him down for medical procedures—but with Georgene, he was a devoted muffin of a creature.

When she got pregnant, Duffy sat beside her and boosted her spirits—not just through her morning sickness, but, she says, through her "morning, noon, and night sickness." Anemic, hypoglycemic, and emotionally wretched, she threw up constantly. Duffy stood loyally beside her in the bathroom, a statue of support.

When she lay on her bed all day feeling weak and discouraged, he cuddled under her chin and stuck with her. Through nine months of suffering, he protected her emotionally until she was finally counting the minutes between contractions. Then he seemed to realize that this pain was different from her previous discomfort. With great sensitivity, he settled on her bed but kept his distance.

After she left for the hospital, Duffy continued standing guard on the kitchen windowsill. He kept up his surveillance for days and refused to eat until she came home with the baby.

• Jim's sixteen-year-old tabby, Watney, earned a string of adjectives as unbecoming as Duffy's nickname, "The Terror." People called her misanthropic, stubborn, irascible, crotchety. And huffy. When Jim brought home a new kitten, Watney showed her displeasure by urinating on his stove burners.

Watney was the quintessential aloof cat until Jim's first wife, Ruth, got colon cancer. After her surgery, the doctors said that they could do no more for her. She came home to die. Watney realized immediately that Ruth needed comfort. The cat climbed on her lap, wriggled to her shoulder, and snuggled against the side of her head. Whenever Ruth became upset or despondent, Watney meowed and purred in her ear to soothe her.

Weeks later when Ruth lay, unconscious, in bed, Watney kept vigil on her pillow. Though Ruth was unresponsive to Jim or her visitors, she smiled and reached her hand up to touch the cat, who made little encouraging squeaks. Whenever Ruth moved or shook with agitation, Watney purred in her ear; and Ruth would relax.

Although she was not present when Ruth finally died, Watney still somehow knew that she was gone. For days the cat refused to go upstairs to Ruth's room. Watney's job of comforting her and escorting her to a peaceful death had been accomplished. Weeks later, the cat resumed her role as surly, misanthropic tiger.

CHAPTER SIX

BEYOND COURAGE
in WATER

ANNETTE MCDONALD adopted Norman, a blond Labrador retriever puppy, on the very day before he was scheduled to be euthanized at a Seaside, Oregon, animal shelter. The pup appeared to be healthy, but when he reached the age of nine months, he began misjudging distances and bumping into doors and furniture. A veterinarian diagnosed an incurable genetic disorder that had caused his retina to deteriorate. Norman would be blind for the rest of his life.

Annette's friends watched him stumble and smash into tables and chairs. "Put him down," they urged. "He's no good to anybody."

"I'd never put him down," she retorted. "Norman is part of my family."

The dog showed great courage. Although some blind dogs become so fearful and depressed that they refuse to take one step alone, Norman seemed to accept his fate and went on with his life in his familiar house and yard. He even enjoyed going to the beach, where the wind ruffled his fur and he could smell the salt and fish in the sea air. He also managed to fetch sticks, by using senses other than sight. When Annette threw a stick for him, he followed her scent on the wood and the "thunk" of the stick hitting the sand.

One afternoon Norman lay on the beach and sniffed the air. In the distance, Lisa Nibley, a teenager, swam out into the ocean with her brother. Although she was a good swimmer, the strong current rapidly pulled her into deep water. She tried to return to shore but could not swim against the tide.

When she yelled for help, people on the beach noticed her but thought she was just playing with her brother. But Norman was alert to something frantic in the pitch and tone of Lisa's voice. He cocked his head, listened, and realized that she was in trouble. Standing up, he headed in the direction of Lisa's shouts. When the cold water hit his shoulders, he started paddling toward her.

Annette watched in amazement from the beach. She hadn't known that her dog could swim. Using Lisa's voice as a beacon, though, he swam farther and farther. Without the security of seeing where he was going, Norman focused only on getting to Lisa. He blinked against the salty waves and strained to keep his head above them. When he finally reached Lisa, she grabbed his fur and he held her up. They splashed and struggled in the waves.

Norman seemed confused about what to do next. As he circled around with Lisa hanging onto him, Annette

could tell that he was trying to figure out in which direction he should swim to get to shore. To help him find his way, she shouted, "Norman! Norman!"

Following Annette's voice, he slowly towed Lisa toward the beach. But then Lisa somehow lost her grip on his fur. As she flailed her arms to keep her head above water, Norman sniffed the air and tried to locate her by scent, but that was impossible. The ocean smells drowned out any trace of Lisa.

Again he circled in the water. Annette knew that he couldn't locate Lisa because he couldn't see her.

"He's blind! Call his name!" she yelled to Lisa. "His name is Norman."

"Norman!" Lisa shouted. "Norman!"

The dog swam to her as quickly as he could and with great effort towed her to shore.

———

PRISCILLA, A three-month-old piglet, lived with Victoria Herberta in Houston, Texas. The piglet wore a purple leash and harness that complemented the three shades of purple paint on the exterior of Herberta's house. All day long Priscilla lay in the yard, soaked up the sun, and listened to the clank of soft-drink cans, hanging by strings to decorate the front porch.

Herberta often strolled around the neighborhood with her piglet on the purple leash. And when not on walks, Priscilla rooted in her own special bed and wading pool and dined on V-8 juice, tuna sandwiches, and pickles. Occasionally, she took drives in the car to the Brazos River, where Herberta wanted to teach her, along with the family dogs, to swim. On the first five trips, Priscilla squealed in protest when Herberta held her in the water. But on the sixth trip, Herberta released her into the river, and Priscilla paddled around with her plump little legs and seemed content.

One hot afternoon soon after this successful swimming lesson, Herberta's friend Carol Burk took Priscilla to swim in Houston's Lake Somerville with Anthony, her eleven-year-old mentally disadvantaged son.

"Stay near shore," Burk told Anthony. "I'll be back in a minute."

He stayed behind and waded in the shallow water while his mother led the piglet farther out for a final quick dip. Priscilla's purple leash floated behind her in the deep water.

Anthony watched his mother and the piglet in the distance. He did not like being left alone. He began wading deeper and deeper toward them, stepped into water that was well over his head, and disappeared from sight. When he came sputtering to the surface, gasping for air, he screamed and waved his arms, then sank again. But Anthony's mother was too far away to help him.

Priscilla, however, was closer. She swam toward the boy.

"Catch hold of her leash!" Burk shouted in alarm.

When Anthony finally grabbed it, he *and* the piglet went under. Burk was certain that they both were going to drown. But seconds later, Priscilla's ears and snout appeared and Anthony was holding onto her.

Priscilla then used all her strength to get Anthony to shore. Weighing just forty-five pounds herself, she dragged the nearly ninety-pound boy almost 150 feet to shallow water.

When Burk related the story about Priscilla's rescue of her son, Herberta was not surprised. Her piglet always responded to a human cry, she said. Priscilla always showed concern and would run—or swim—to help anyone in trouble.

STORIES OF creatures rescuing people from drowning are among the most common examples of animal compassion. Even if the animals are wary of water—or hate it—they will often ignore their fear and jump in anyway to help.

Animals have shown great inventiveness in their methods of getting people to safety. One dog swam out of a flooded culvert with a little boy on his back. Another dog let a teenage girl grab her choke-chain collar, then tugged her free of quicksand and towed her to a pond's bank. Yet another grabbed a woman's hair in his teeth and dragged her from underneath an overturned raft; then, as she held onto his tail, he pulled her through the river rapids to shore.

POUDRE SAT on an isolated bank downstream from a dam on Colorado's Cache La Poudre River. The golden retriever raised an eyelid and lazily watched Dale Windsor cast a green-woolly-worm fly into the water. If Poudre had had her way, she would have jumped into the river and paddled back and forth. But Windsor had forbidden her to do so. Fish were spawning in the river's sandy beds; if Poudre played in the water, she'd disturb them.

Though she always willingly obeyed him, she gazed with longing at the river. Then she resumed her job of guarding Windsor, a task she took extremely seriously, especially since his back surgery the previous year.

After he'd caught two fish, a third one bit off the fly and swam away. Windsor had to climb one hundred yards up a steep granite mountain to his truck in order to get another fly from his tackle box. The rocky slope was muddy and slick from rain the night before. Cautiously, the man and his dog inched their way along.

After Windsor got his fly, he started back down to the river with Poudre. Suddenly he slipped, crashed on his right arm, and tumbled headfirst down the granite slope. As he rolled toward the water, he hit his head and gashed his body on the rocks. Landing face-down in the river, he fainted.

Poudre rushed over, bit into his fishing vest, and rolled him onto his back, so he would not drown. Then using her teeth, she dragged him to a shallow pool between two rocks where he'd be safe. When he regained consciousness, she was hovering over him with a questioning look in her eyes. She cocked her head, as if waiting for further instructions.

Windsor blinked, conscious but uncomprehending. Every inch of his body hurt. Where was he? What had happened? His face was cut and bloody. His back-surgery incision had ripped open. His right arm and wrist were shattered. He could not move.

Then he remembered why he'd *better* move: At any moment the gates of the dam might be opened and the river would come flooding down on him. With his broken right arm, he couldn't swim, and he was too injured to walk out of the water. Surely, he would drown, and no one would even find him.

Fear chilled him. He looked up at Poudre, standing beside him. Asking her to help him would not be fair. Though he knew she would give all she had for him, she was not strong enough to drag him all the way up the hill to his truck. At six-foot-three, he outweighed her by one hundred pounds. But she was his only hope of staying alive.

"Come, girl," Windsor said. "You're going to have to pull me up the mountain."

Poudre knew what "pull" meant; he had once made a little sled and harness for her to haul neighborhood children around. She moved close enough for Windsor to grasp her collar with his good hand and then pulled him to a sitting position. After he rested for a moment, she again pulled with all her strength as he used his left elbow to help move himself along. Slowly and painfully, she managed to drag him out of the water and up the rock about ten feet.

"You've got to help me more," he told her.

She mustered her strength and tugged him a few more feet. Blood poured from her mouth. Hauling so much weight just by her collar put too much pressure on her neck. No matter how eager she was to help Windsor, she could not continue this way or she'd die.

"We've got to do this differently," Windsor moaned.

He hooked his belt around her chest to harness her. Then he gripped the belt with his good hand, and she dug her nails into the rock and pulled again. For a long, agonizing hour, she crawled around trees, bushes, and boulders up to the truck, where Windsor, exhausted and in terrible pain, passed out again.

When he opened his eyes, Poudre was sitting beside him, watching his face intently. Though *she* was also worn out and bruised, she was still waiting to help him. But there wasn't much more she could do. On such a deserted road, no one was likely to come along, either. Windsor tried to clear his mind enough to figure out how to help himself.

He couldn't drive to a hospital, he decided, because he'd have to leave Poudre in the truck. On such a warm day, she'd suffocate in the cab. And someone might steal her if he left her in the open bed. Somehow he had to get her home. From there his wife, Virginia, could drive him to the hospital.

Windsor gathered his strength and forced himself to stand. With his left arm, he got Poudre into the truck bed, then walked, shaking, to the cab, and got behind the wheel. By reaching his left hand across his body, he managed to turn the key in the ignition. In the same way, he shifted his standard transmission and drove slowly down the dirt road. After thirty minutes, he again became dizzy and weak.

Worried that he might faint, he pulled over to the side of the road. Now he needed Poudre more than ever, he realized—not for physical help, but for comfort and emotional support. Windsor climbed unsteadily out of the truck and brought her up to the cab beside him. To avoid passing out, he talked to her, and she listened and observed him. For the next fifty-five miles, her loving presence kept him going.

Just five miles from home, Windsor felt so weak and sick that he had to pull over again, and he passed out a third time. When he regained consciousness, Poudre was nuzzling him and licking his face to encourage him. He started the motor and, with extreme difficulty, managed to keep the car on the road. But he wove back and forth across the lanes.

Windsor finally pulled up to his house and honked his horn to call Virginia. "I've been hurt bad." Speaking caused more pain. "I need to go to the emergency room."

Poudre willingly followed Virginia to the house. The dog seemed to know that her job was done. Virginia rushed Windsor to the hospital, where doctors x-rayed his broken ribs, bandaged his head wounds, and stitched up his ripped surgical incision. Windsor was more than lucky to be alive, and he knew that he owed his life to Poudre.

When he telephoned home from the hospital, Virginia held the receiver to Poudre's ear, so he could thank her for rescuing him. At the sound of his voice, she whined and squeaked with pleasure. To cheer Windsor, Virginia brought the dog to the hospital. When Poudre saw how pale and vulnerable he was, she whimpered with such distress that even the nurses noticed tears flowing from her eyes.

She ran, limping, around the room. She'd over-extended herself tugging Windsor up the mountain and had torn the muscles in her hind legs, the veterinarian later explained. Nothing could be done to repair them; they would never heal.

For the rest of her life, Poudre would be stiff and sore. Every day she would suffer because she'd ignored her own safety in order to save the man she loved. Twice a day, she would have to take pain medication. Yet no matter how great her pain, she still insisted on following Windsor everywhere he went.

CHAPTER SEVEN

CARING
STRAYS

G O TO Sinai Hospital. Talk with the emergency
room doctors." The dispatcher sounded worried over the patrol-car radio of Detroit policemen Joe
Dabliz and Timothy Bannon. "A woman just arrived
there. She may have had a baby. The baby's not at the
hospital."

Dabliz's stomach lurched. Was the dispatcher saying that some crazy woman had given birth and killed
her baby? Dabliz had two children whom he adored,
and he could not imagine any parent committing such
an unspeakable crime. But sometimes people could be
savages.

Dabliz knew this call might lead to one of those savages, especially after he and Bannon arrived at the hospital and talked with a doctor. An ambulance had
brought the woman, hemorrhaging, to Sinai about 10:45
that morning. After the doctor had examined her, he

determined that she'd given birth to a full-term baby about an hour earlier.

"She denies ever being pregnant." He shook his head in disbelief. "And nobody brought in the baby."

Now Dabliz and Bannon had to find out what had happened to it.

"We're investigating an animal, not a human mother," Dabliz said bitterly, as they drove to the woman's house.

It was a neat, tidy dwelling in a quiet neighborhood. They left their patrol car and walked up the sidewalk through a well-kept yard to the front porch. The woman's mother answered the door.

"Did your daughter just have a baby?" Dabliz asked.

"My God, no." She raised her eyebrows with genuine surprise that he would even ask. "My daughter got sick this morning. She was bleeding in the bathroom and tracked blood all over the house. But she didn't have a baby."

"Can we come in and look?"

"Sure."

Dabliz and Bannon found blood spattered all around the bathroom. But a full-term baby, they realized, could never have been flushed down the toilet. A trail of blood drops, each drop about a foot apart, led to the kitchen, then through a side door and out of the house.

While Bannon checked upstairs, Dabliz followed the blood trail down several steps and along the driveway to the back fence. A dense puddle of red had collected on that spot because, he suspected, the woman had stopped a moment before climbing over the fence into the alley.

Dabliz bent down and examined the drops more closely. A chill came over him as he imagined the horror of what must have happened.

His heart seemed to stop.

Dabliz braced himself for the worst. The dead baby's body would be stuffed in a garbage can in the alley. Or buried somehow. Or perhaps the woman had tossed the infant into a passing garbage truck. No matter what she did, the crime was hideous.

When he raised his eyes from the blood drops and glanced down the alley, his gaze locked with the gentle brown eyes of a stray dog. She had the pointed nose of a German shepherd, but was a little smaller and had long, filthy, matted fur. She was also pitifully thin; her ribs stuck out like thick raised stripes around her chest. She had obviously been living on the streets for a long time and was in great need of love and care.

The dog lay with her body curled protectively around a baby, which she was licking with great tenderness. The baby's skin was pink and fresh; the stray had cleaned away the mother's blood. The dog cuddled the infant, who seemed to be reaching out for reassurance. In the baby's hand was a little twig.

"My God!" Dabliz shouted. "Tim! Tim! Come here!"

Bannon tore out of the house.

"She threw away the baby!" Dabliz could not believe what he was seeing. "She threw away the baby!"

While Bannon dashed to the car, Dabliz jumped over the fence and picked up the baby, a boy, still wet from the stray dog's saliva. Though she seemed to realize that Dabliz would help the baby, not harm him, she watched intently, ready to jump on Dabliz and fight him off if necessary.

Dabliz took off his bullet-proof vest and wrapped it around the child, then warmed him under his shirt.

"Don't worry," Dabliz told the dog. "The baby will be all right. You did a good job. You were a wonderful mother."

The stray cocked her head at the compliments, but her face looked bedraggled and pathetic. She belonged in front of a cozy fireplace, not out on the cold, dirty pavement. She deserved to have a family fussing over her instead of being all alone against the world.

The police car roared down the alley. Bannon slammed on the brakes just a few feet from the stray. She jumped back to avoid being hit, as she must have done many times in order to survive on the streets. Dabliz got into the car with the baby. As Bannon pressed on the gas and sped down the alley, Dabliz turned around to take one last look at the dog.

Dignified and calm, she watched the car until it was out of sight. But her eyes were sad and dejected.

Tears rolled down Dabliz's cheeks as he handed the baby to an emergency room doctor. The day's events had been too emotional for him—an unwanted baby's death prevented by an unwanted dog. Dabliz was relieved to learn that the baby, despite suffering from hypothermia, would be fine.

But the dog—surely *she* wouldn't be fine. She would be wandering around hungry, except for what garbage cans dished out to her, and cold, if she couldn't find a sheltered place to sleep. Dabliz agonized because he'd had to take the baby from her. He was to blame if the stray was sad about losing the baby. Perhaps she'd wanted it for a friend.

When Dabliz found himself having these thoughts, he knew he was losing his perspective; of course, a stray dog could not successfully raise a baby on the streets. Nevertheless, his heart went out in sympathy for the lonely, goodhearted dog.

Later that day, Dabliz went back to the alley to search for her. He returned to that spot several times in the next few weeks, but he never found her. He was devastated.

"Who knows what happened to that wonderful dog?" he still asks himself. Someone had thrown *her* away as surely as the mother had thrown away her baby. Each event was a tragedy.

STRAY DOGS often carry out amazing rescues. They seem to be drawn to people who are in need and arrive just in time to offer help. Although they have no allegiance to anyone or anything, they are capable of displaying great compassion for people they've never even seen before. The animals have nothing to gain by extending themselves—and yet they do it.

• When Austrian mountain guide Armin Liedl was leading four Germans up Aconcagua, a 23,000-foot mountain in the Andes, all the men knew that the trip was dangerous. Getting to the summit had claimed the lives of many climbers. All the same, the men slogged higher and higher.

They were surprised when a dog suddenly appeared out of nowhere, quite a distance from any village. He tagged along with them, wandered off, then returned. When Liedl found him shivering in the snow outside his tent one morning, he knew then that the dog belonged to no one. Liedl felt sorry for the stray and fed him.

Several days later, as Liedl and two of the men climbed to 21,000 feet, the dog barked and whined to get their attention. Suspecting that something was wrong, Liedl made his way over to the stray. Lying beside him were the group's other two men, lost and suffering from altitude sickness. The dog was clearly concerned about their safety. And without the dog's warning, Liedl never would have known they needed help.

The stray seemed to have arrived specifically to alert the climbers to danger and possibly to save the two men's lives. Once the dog had escorted the group safely to Aconcagua's peak, he vanished as silently as he had appeared.

• Late one night, as Nils Haugejorden crunched through the snow in Alberta, Canada, he slipped and injured himself so severely that he could not stand. Lying, helpless and alone, in the subzero blizzard, he was sure he'd freeze to death before anyone found him the next morning.

A stray dog silently crept over and cuddled up to him. By licking Haugejorden's face, the stray comforted him and kept him alert. The dog stopped his ministrations only long enough to bark at neighboring houses to summon help. Finally, the noise woke someone who came outside and discovered Haugejorden. An ambulance rushed him to the hospital, where he was treated for severe frostbite. In gratitude, he adopted the stray and named him Lonesome.

· When Indiana farmer William Foy was assembling a tractor lift in his barn, a metal bracket slipped, crashed down on him, and pinned him, scarcely able to breathe, under the tractor. Inside Foy's house, his son Billy heard nothing of this accident. But the family's cocker spaniel did.

The dog dashed to the window, whined, and barked so persistently that Billy let him out and followed him to the barn. They found Foy, still trapped under the machinery. Billy tried several times to free him and finally raised the bracket with a floor jack. Without the cocker spaniel, Foy might have lain there, unable to move, for many hours.

Until the family had adopted him only three days earlier, the dog had been a stray.

———

LATE ONE chilly afternoon, Josh Carlyle, a ten-year-old child with Down's syndrome, saw two stray mutts—one mostly dachshund and the other mostly blue heeler—hanging around his rural Missouri home. Fascinated by the dogs, he followed them into the rugged Ozark woods and realized too late that he did not know the way home.

When Josh's mother looked out her kitchen window to call him for supper, the boy was nowhere in sight. She went outside, shouting his name, and searched the neighborhood but could not find him. Frightened, she telephoned Sheriff Ralph Hendrix, who came immediately. As the sky darkened and the temperature fell, Hendrix knew he had a crisis on his hands.

He parked his sky-blue school bus down the hill from Josh's house and set up a command post for the search. Within a few hours, three hundred volunteers, who had heard on Hendrix's scanner that Josh was missing, showed up to help. Reserve deputies arrived. Tracking dogs were brought in from neighboring counties. All night long Hendrix sent teams of eight to ten people to comb the hills, fingertip-to-fingertip, for Josh.

When he hadn't been found by the next morning, Hendrix tried not to feel discouraged. Yet he couldn't help but fear that Josh might be dead. He sent out more volunteers and asked them to search not only the woods, but also the caves and cliff ledges. By the second night, the temperature had fallen to below zero, and no one had found any trace of Josh except for one boot-print. Hendrix was worried that Josh had frozen to death overnight.

"Go north. Unless you find Josh, don't come back till dark," Hendrix told searchers on horseback the next morning.

One of the men, Oscar Nell, rode into the woods. When he tugged his horse's reins to direct him up a hill, the horse balked and insisted on turning down toward a hollow. Nell decided that the horse might know more than *he* did about Josh's whereabouts, and he let the horse lead.

Nell heard a dog barking and squinted through the distant trees in the direction of the sound. A blue heeler mutt was yapping and running up and down a steep hill; then it stopped and panted. Nell was certain that the dog was trying to get his attention.

He followed the dog deeper into the woods and discovered Josh lying on the ground. Huddled next to him was the stray dachshund.

"Josh! Josh!" Nell leaped off his horse and ran toward the boy.

The blue heeler snapped and growled at him so fiercely that Nell stopped cold. Though the stray had tried to make Nell follow him, now he appeared to consider the man a threat. Nell talked softly to the stray and tried to make his voice sound gentle, but compelling. The mutt was still reluctant to trust him but finally quit barking and seemed less inclined to bite.

When the boy raised his head, Nell was immensely relieved to see that he was still alive. Nell helped him to a sitting position and propped him against a tree.

"Are you hungry?" Nell asked.

Josh was too cold and frightened to respond.

Nell gave him a sandwich, but Josh's chattering teeth prevented him from eating. His mouth was bloody. He was covered with dirt and bits of leaves and grass. But his face was clean, though chapped in spots where the dachshund stray had licked him.

Nell helped Josh drink a little water, put him on the horse, and climbed on the saddle behind him. As the horse headed back to the search team command post, the strays protectively followed.

Then Nell had to stop his horse. Josh's toes had been frostbitten to blisters; the jostling caused too much pain for him to go on. Nell made a temporary camp and built a fire.

"I'll bring back help," he promised.

As he rode off, the dogs moved closer to Josh. They guarded and warmed him until the rescue party returned in a Jeep to take him to a helicopter.

They carefully laid him on the back seat and sped down the road. The dogs barked and howled, clearly upset that Josh was leaving. The dachshund chased after the car until she could no longer keep up on her squat little legs.

Later, the strays apparently split up and wandered back to Josh's house to look for him. A search-and-rescue volunteer picked up the dachshund; Josh's next-door neighbors found the heeler on a nearby hill and put out food to lure him closer. After a veterinarian examined the strays and determined that they were healthy, Josh's parents agreed to adopt them.

The afternoon the dogs were to join their new family, Hendrix brought them to greet Josh on his release from the hospital. The dogs, wild with excitement to see Josh again, tugged at their leads. Josh was thrilled.

The dachshund leaped onto Josh's wheelchair, licked him, and whimpered. The heeler, more reserved, sniffed Josh from head to toe to make certain that he was safe.

Their obvious devotion deeply moved Hendrix. "The Lord had them stay with Josh and take care of him," the sheriff said. "His surviving was a miracle."

A miracle made possible by the compassion of two strays.

———

DAVID BRUCE pushed his two-year-old son, David Jr, in his stroller to St. Bede's Church in Hayward, California. What might have been a pleasant outing with his child was decidedly not; they were going to the church to accept a charity meal. Bruce had recently been laid off as a warehouse worker. Though he'd been looking for a new job, he had not found one yet. He felt insecure and troubled.

As he and David walked along the sidewalk of a busy two-lane street, a stray rottweiler mutt stepped in front of them. She was pathetic—and appeared as insecure and troubled as Bruce felt. Her bony ribs stuck out beneath scruffy brown fur that had not been washed in many months. As she lowered her head and stared at the concrete, Bruce could see that she lacked confidence.

Eager to pet the pitiful dog, David begged Bruce to let him out of the stroller. The mutt seemed harmless enough, Bruce decided. He lifted his son and set him on the sidewalk. As Bruce stooped for a moment to tie his shoe, David stepped off the curb and darted into the street. Frantic, Bruce straightened up and ran after him.

A blue sedan sped toward David, who was blocked from the driver's view by a parked car. Bruce was too

far away to grab his son. As the sedan zoomed closer, Bruce tensed with terror.

Bruce screamed and ran toward David, but the stray dog got to him first. She jumped on the boy and shoved him out of the car's way just as the driver saw them and slammed on his brakes. The car screeched to a stop only inches from the spot where David had been standing.

The stray sat protectively beside David, wagged her tail, panted, and begged Bruce with sad brown eyes to pay attention to her. Still shaking, he picked up his son and put him back into the stroller. Then he bent down and patted and thanked the dog.

She was so hungry for affection that she affixed herself to Bruce. She tagged along with them to the church, waited patiently until they emerged, and then followed them home. As she shuffled along, she seemed desperate for more attention. Bruce stooped and stroked her ears. He named her Minnie.

After her brave rescue of his son, Bruce felt greatly indebted to Minnie. He could not bear to imagine her running the streets and starving again. Though he wanted her to be his friend for life, he knew that he could not keep her. He lived in an apartment with restrictions against pets; his landlord would never break the rules and let Bruce offer the dog a permanent home.

With no job and no money to finance a move to another building, he had to give up Minnie. Guilt gnawed at him as he called the Hayward Animal Shelter; an officer soon came and took Minnie away. Bruce vowed to himself that her incarceration would be only temporary and that he would find her former owners. He was determined to do right by her.

The shelter staff fed, washed, and brushed Minnie. They tried to make her more appealing, so that someone would adopt her. Day after day she sat in her cage, wagged her tail, and peered eagerly out at the families who visited the shelter. But none of them chose her because she was just an average-looking mutt. The families wanted a handsome dog, not Minnie.

Bruce was certain that Minnie's original family had lost her and was looking for her. How could they possibly have abandoned her? She was such an exceptional dog. Realizing that Minnie could not stay at the shelter forever, Bruce reported her to every veterinarian in the area. When no one contacted him to claim her, he was crestfallen.

To add to his anxiety, three weeks after Minnie was taken in at the shelter, the building had to be vacated, so that new floors could be installed. Since temporary homes could not be found for all the shelter's dogs, some of them would have to be destroyed. That meant that the most attractive dogs—the ones most likely to be adopted—would be allowed to live. Minnie would be one of the first to die.

More distressed than ever, Bruce gave up trying to track down Minnie's original family and just looked for a good home for her. Since by then he'd found a job, he offered to pay the fifty-dollar adoption fee if only a family would take her. Time was running out. But there were no volunteers.

Minnie, of course, did not realize that she was in danger. She continued to sit in her cage, wag her tail, and gaze at visitors with longing eyes. Though she'd eaten enough lately to gain a little weight, her backbone still jutted out in a ridge that offended petting hands. The clumps of fur she'd lost from malnutrition had not yet grown back. The shelter's visitors glanced at her with indifference and walked away.

Death loomed over her like an iron roof. Desperate, Bruce called local newspapers and television stations. He described Minnie's plight to reporters and begged them to find someone who would be as compassionate toward the stray as she'd been toward his son. After his appeal, Minnie's story was publicized.

The next morning before the shelter opened, forty-five messages from people eager to adopt her jammed the telephone answering machine. In the next few days over one hundred more callers expressed interest in giving her a home. The shelter sifted through the offers and invited Annie Urbanos and her five-year-old son Nicholas to meet Minnie in the shelter's "get acquainted room." Minnie leaped on Nicholas with such joy that she nearly knocked him over. She licked his face and hands, then pressed herself against Urbanos as if the woman were more important than food or oxygen.

"How could a dog who's suffered so much be so loving?" Urbanos asked the shelter volunteers. "She's a wonderful dog. We'd give anything to have her."

And so they got her.

In a real home at last, Minnie explored the rugs with grateful sniffs. But she was obviously still terrified of being dumped on the streets again. From stress and worry, all of the fur on her tail fell out, exposing her pink, vulnerable skin. But gradually, the family's love nurtured Minnie into the healthy dog she was meant to be.

She became plump and, finally, confident. Fluffy fur grew back on her tail. In a roundabout way her good deed was rewarded. The stray dog's kindness to a stranger led her to a loving home.

CHAPTER EIGHT

PROTECTION *from* FIRE

For Christmas, Paula Howton of Grand Rivers, Kentucky, bought her mother a teacup Pomeranian. The dog reminded Paula of a miniature fox. She had bright eyes, a pointed nose, a bushy tail, and red fur that fluffed and flopped around her body like a dust mop. She also had tiny pointed teeth, like little needles, that she occasionally sank into people's ankles. As an adult, she stood less than six inches tall and weighed just a pound and a half.

Paula gave her the Native American name Shukota and brought her to her mother as a present.

The minute her mother, Betty, saw Shukota, she narrowed her eyes and asked, "How much did that dog cost?"

"Five hundred dollars," Paula answered.

"Five hundred dollars!" Betty was indignant. "I could have spent that much on something a lot better than that dog."

Betty never let Paula forget that she'd wasted her money. Five hundred dollars for a mouse of a canine was beyond extravagance. Whenever Paula didn't have enough money to buy something, Betty reminded her of her poor judgment. "You could buy it if you hadn't paid five hundred dollars for that dog."

"That dog" apparently picked up the waves of disapproval. She sulked. She wouldn't have anything to do with Betty. Shukota hid under chairs, would not come when called, and looked through Betty as if she were invisible.

Paula finally admitted to herself that this gift to her mother had been a failure and brought Shukota to her own house. Soon Paula became attached to Shukota, who, in turn, became highly protective of Paula. Whenever anyone came too close to Paula, Shukota puffed up to her full six inches and grew ferocious. The dog attacked her share of feet.

Several years later, Betty and Paula—along with Paula's nephew Charlie and her Aunt Cookie—drove a Winnebago to Mexico to buy blankets for an import business that the family intended to start. Traveling with them were Shukota—who by then had grown more tolerant of Betty—and Token, a standard Pomeranian, who weighed three pounds.

The family bought their future business inventory, along with many rounds of ammunition for Betty's guns, her favorite hobby. Then they climbed into their Winnebago and headed back north. Betty drove while Aunt Cookie dozed in the front passenger seat, and Paula and Charlie napped with the dogs on a bed in the rear. The November day was sunny and mild. The mobile home soon filled with contented snores.

Sixty miles across the U.S. border, Shukota began yapping. Paula woke and tried to quiet her before she disturbed Aunt Cookie and Charlie. No such luck. Shukota continued to bark as loud as her tiny lungs could manage. The yaps were as piercing as lasers. Aunt Cookie snapped open her eyes.

"What's *wrong* with that dog?" Betty demanded. (To Betty, Shukota was still "that dog.") "What have you done to her? Did you roll over on her?"

"No," Paula said.

Shukota yapped even more. She threw all of her energy into trying to communicate. Then she suddenly grew silent, drew her head back, and closed her eyes.

"Something's wrong with her, Mama. I think she's having convulsions. Pull over. Hurry." Paula hugged Shukota closer.

Paula turned around to check on Token; he and Charlie were curled up, asleep. From under the bed, black smoke billowed as a flame shot out from the heater vent. Shukota, trying to warn the family that their Winnebago was on fire, had worked herself into a frenzy. Now the dog was sick from inhaling smoke.

"Pull over!" Paula shouted at Betty again. "We're on fire. Pull over!"

Betty slammed on the brakes at the side of the highway and jumped out of the motor home.

Paula handed Shukota and Token to Aunt Cookie. "Take the dogs and get out of here!"

Paula dragged Charlie, half asleep, out of bed and to the Winnebago's door. She pushed him onto the road. "Run as fast as you can."

Outside, Betty gave Shukota mouth-to-mouth resuscitation and was able to revive her. Inside, Paula grabbed clothes and blankets and tossed them out the door.

When Paula tried to return for another load, Betty held her arm. "Don't go in there," she warned. "The Winnebago's going to burn."

As Aunt Cookie and Charlie ran down the road with the dogs, Paula and her mother backed away from the motor home—just in time. The gas tanks blasted like thunder. Windows shattered. Flames leaped toward the sky. As smoke blackened the air, Betty's ammunition exploded like fire crackers. In seconds, the motor home became a charred, empty metal shell.

Flames heated Paula's face, but the rest of her body was icy with fear. Without Shukota's warning, she and her family would have been trapped inside the Winnebago and burned alive. Shaken, Paula stood staring at the ashes. She could have so easily become ashes herself, but only her hands were burned.

Ambulances, fire trucks, and highway patrol cars quickly arrived. Paramedics hastened over to her.

"You have to go to the hospital," one of them said. "You need a doctor to bandage your hands."

Paula refused to leave her teacup dog behind. "If she's good enough to save my life, she's good enough to go with me."

The paramedics saw her point and allowed the dogs to accompany Paula. As the ambulance sped away, Paula looked out the back window. The rubble of the Winnebago shrank to a dark, distant speck beside the road.

The fire had burned four thousand dollars in cash and the equivalent value in blankets. Paula had lost not only her belongings, but also her hopes for starting a business. Yet she could not complain: Her family—and her dogs—were safe, thanks to Shukota. Paula was more grateful to the tiny creature than she could ever express.

"Is she worth five hundred dollars now?" Paula later asked her mother at the hospital.

"Yes," Betty admitted. She had never had such an easy time eating crow.

Months later a stranger approached Paula and Betty and began petting Shukota. "I'd really like to buy your dog," he said. "Is she for sale?"

"For sale?!" Betty retorted, indignant. "That dog saved our lives. I wouldn't sell her for a million dollars."

HUNDREDS OF dogs and cats have warned people of fires. When the blaze has started in the middle of the night, the animals have used every possible means to wake their human families and get them to safety.

• Donald and Rose Sylvester, in Lowell, Massachusetts, were awakened by their mongrel, Blackie, barking like a maniac to warn them that a vacant house across the street was burning. Oddly, just a few weeks later on Christmas night, their *own* apartment caught on fire. Yapping, Blackie charged from room to room. He nuzzled the sleeping children and tugged their hair with his teeth to rouse them—just in time for all ten family members and their guests to escape.

• In *Pet Heroes* by Paul Simons, Samantha, a black Burmese cat in Rancho Mirage, California, leaped on the bed of Francesca and Robert Goldbraith, meowed, grabbed their sheet in her mouth, and tried to yank it off. When they finally opened their eyes and found their bedroom filled with smoke, they called the fire department, then rushed to wake the other tenants in their apartment building. The fire, which had started in the basement, spread rapidly down the block. Samantha's desperate pulling at her owners' sheet had saved forty-four people.

ONE SUMMER night, a heavy storm hit New Bern, North Carolina, as Rosevelt and Linda Matthews were sleeping. Blue-white lightning zigzagged through the sky, and thunder rolled like kettle drums.

A resounding boom woke Linda. Terrified, she jumped out of bed. "Did you hear that?" she asked Rosevelt. "What was it?"

"Maybe lightning struck the TV." Still half asleep, Rosevelt tossed back his covers, stumbled across the bedroom, and unplugged the television.

He climbed back into bed, and they tried to fall asleep again. But in addition to the storm, the faint sound of a dog's barking outside kept them awake. It seemed to be coming from Roc, their year-old rottweiler–Chesapeake Bay retriever mix, who had always been a supremely conscientious watchdog. For him, the barking seemed unusually weak.

"You think that's Roc?" Linda asked.

"The barking's too far away," Rosevelt said. "It's got to be some dog down the street."

The barking got louder.

"That *is* Roc. There must be a prowler outside."

Rosevelt looked out the window into the backyard, where Roc was standing in the rain, looking up at him. Roc, clearly upset about something, continued his deep, rumbling barks, but there appeared to be no one else in the yard.

"No prowler," Rosevelt reassured Linda.

She wasn't convinced. When Rosevelt returned to bed, she went to the window to check for herself. Roc was running back and forth from the side yard to the back of the house. As he wore a muddy path in the grass, his barks became more urgent.

"Don't worry. He's just scared of the thunder," Rosevelt said.

"That doesn't make sense. Roc's been in plenty of storms. He's never been afraid of thunder before."

He'd also never become this worked up without a good reason. Maybe Roc had hurt himself, Linda worried. Maybe he was sick.

Rosevelt got up again and walked around inside the house to check for problems. When he found nothing amiss, he returned to bed—and Roc continued to bark.

As rain pounded the window, Linda worried. Unable to get comfortable, she tossed between the sheets. The minute it was light, she told herself, she'd go out and check on Roc to make sure nothing was wrong with him. She wished that it was light already.

The doorbell rang. Linda and Rosevelt bolted up in bed. Out the window they saw orange flames.

They woke their sons, called the fire department, and tore outside. In the rain, they watched part of their burning roof collapse exactly where they'd been trying to sleep.

Lightning had struck the roof and hit electrical wires in the attic. The wires had started a silent, nearly smoke-free fire. Without the sound of flames popping and crack-ling, Linda and Rosevelt had had no way of knowing that they were in danger. If they'd stayed in bed, their burning ceiling would have crashed down, killing them instantly.

"Who rang at the door to get us up in time?" They asked themselves for the rest of the night.

The next morning they found the answer: Roc's muddy paw print covered the doorbell.

DO ANIMALS warn people of fires just so they them-selves can get outside to safety? Are their rescues acts of self-interest or compassion?

• Budweiser, an adolescent St. Bernard, was lying in the yard when a blast exploded inside the house of Mrs. B. M. Carter in John's Island, South Carolina. He jumped up and barreled through the door to look for Carter and her six grandchildren. Budweiser grabbed the youngest, age four, by her shirt and pulled her through the flames to a neighbor's yard. Then he went back for the five-year-old child, whom he led out by the arm to safety.

By this time, Mrs. Carter had taken her other four grandchildren to the street. But Budweiser refused to stay outside with them. He turned around and started toward the door again to try to save the family's Chihuahua. Unfortunately, the fire's heat was so intense that he had to turn back—just minutes before the roof collapsed and flattened the house to smoldering embers.

• King, a German shepherd mutt, was sleeping when a fire started in the utility room of Mr. and Mrs. Howard Carlson in Granite Falls, Washington. Beside his bed were sliding glass doors that were always left open, so he could go outside. But he did not leave the house to escape the fire. Instead, he clawed and chewed through a plywood door into the burning utility room until his mouth was full of splinters.

He then wriggled through the hole and gashed his back on the ragged plywood. As he bolted through the flames to the bedroom of the Carlsons' daughter, he burned his paws as well. In spite of all of these injuries, he whined and nudged the girl awake, then ran to her parents' bedroom. Because Mr. Carlson had a lung condition, he could not hasten outside as quickly as his wife and daughter. King chose to stay with him. As the house burned around them, they slowly made their way outdoors together.

• On the night before Thanksgiving, Sam, an Oregon cat, watched Mae Udovitch put a turkey in the oven, climb into bed, and fall asleep. At 2:30 A.M., the house filled with smoke. Sam jumped on Udovitch, pawed her hair, squawked, and meowed. When the woman finally opened her eyes, she saw the smoke and rushed to the kitchen, where the turkey was burning.

She ran to the front door and put Sam outside, where he'd be safe, but left the door open in order to let out the smoke. In the kitchen she beat back the flames with towels and happened to glance at the floor: Sam had come back inside. He stood there with an anxious expression. Only after Udovitch had extinguished the fire did he walk out the front door. Udovitch was certain that he wanted to be sure of her safety before he left her.

• Duke, a collie, sat beside Penny Grantz, age ten, as she burned papers in her backyard in Niles, Ohio. Suddenly, a gust of wind carrying red hot cinders billowed her skirt. It burst into flames. Penny ran screaming toward the house for her father. But Duke seemed to realize that she did not have time to reach him.

Before she reached the door, Duke dashed over, grabbed her burning skirt in his teeth, tore and pawed it off her, and badly burned his mouth. The fire spread to her blouse just as her father rushed out and ripped it off her. Penny had to stay in the hospital burn unit for nine weeks; doctors said that without Duke's help, she would surely have died. Duke recuperated at home, where his burned mouth gradually healed.

CHAPTER NINE

TAKING *the* HIT

A T DAWN Benji, an ancient mutt who resembled
Walt Disney's Benji, followed eighty-eight-
year-old Clarence Lea out onto his enclosed porch in
Portland, Indiana. Clarence intended to let Benji out for
his morning walk; but when the elderly man reached for
the outside door, he slipped on snow that had blown
through the crack under the door. As he fell to the floor,
he hit his head. The blow knocked him out.

Although the porch was enclosed, its temperature
was subzero. The wind kept whipping more snow
under the door. Clarence, lying on the floor in just a
light sweater over his shirt and pants, was in serious
danger of freezing to death. As he slipped in and out of
consciousness, Benji came to rescue him.

At three o'clock the next afternoon, Clarence's son
David, who lived across the street, heard the postman
pass by earlier than usual. David went out to the road to

get the mail. To save his father a trip to the mailbox, David took Clarence's letters to his house.

Peering through the window of the enclosed porch, David saw his father sprawled on the floor, nearly dead, his clothes and hair frozen. His skin was blue, and his hands were severely frostbitten. Though conscious, he was too chilled to move.

Huddled between his head and the door was Benji, his fur frozen in spikes. He, too, was nearly dead. Since dawn the dog had lain in front of the door and blocked the crack, so that more snow would not be blown onto Clarence. The dog was so old that he could barely move his arthritic bones, but for ten hours he had kept Clarence from freezing to death.

———

WHEN PEOPLE are in danger, animals have been known to take the hit for them. The creatures seem not just willing, but even eager to use their bodies as a protective shield. Once, a swarm of yellow jackets flew toward twenty-month-old Cassandra Vance in Nashville, Illinois. Sheba, an Alaskan malamute, jumped on her and covered her with his body. Cassandra toddled away with just one sting, but the yellow jackets stung Sheba twenty-seven times. He almost died.

———

URSULA TAIT of Alberta, Canada, set out to hike in the mountains one morning with her Bernese mountain dogs—Balloo and Jessie—and her friend Nina Hofer. Late that afternoon they stopped to rest at the top of a steep climb. Since Tait had a headache, they decided to return home. Tait stood up and called the dogs; then, without warning, she fainted and tumbled down the embankment.

As she rolled faster and faster toward rocks and a huge tree, Hofer stood petrified, unable to stop her. In just seconds Tait would slam into the tree and be killed.

Balloo understood her danger. He leaped up and dashed after her. With great effort he passed her, turned around, and *threw himself in front of her.* She crashed into him so hard that he was thrown back, but he broke her fall just inches from the tree.

Tait lay unconscious and bleeding from cuts on her legs, back, and head. Balloo hovered over her, nudged her, panted—and ignored his own pain and bruises. By the time Hofer reached Balloo and Tait, the injured girl had regained consciousness; but her back hurt, and she had no sensation in her legs. Tait and Hofer decided to stay where they were until someone sent a rescue team.

As the sky darkened, the temperature dropped to thirty-seven degrees, and rain began to fall. Hofer built a fire. Again Balloo shielded Tait, this time from the cold, as he and Jessie snuggled up to her. They left only occasionally to bark for help or to answer the howls of coyotes and wolves.

At sunrise, rescuers sent by the girls' parents spotted Hofer's fire and radioed for a helicopter to take Tait to the hospital. Balloo and Jessie's barks seemed to urge the team to hurry. Doctors discovered that Tait had cracked two vertebrae, which would heal in time. In the future, whenever those vertebrae ached, she reminded herself how much worse off she'd have been if Balloo had not thrown his body between her and the tree.

WHEN A car bomb exploded behind Brian McMullan's house in Belfast, Ireland, his twelve-year-old terrier-Labrador mutt, Bruno, was traumatized. The bomb blasted with such violence that McMullan was thrown from his backyard into his kitchen. Bruno cut his paws on flying glass and was forever wary of explosives.

He surely remembered that horrible event when teenage thugs threw firecrackers over the wall of his backyard for several days. Five different times Bruno barked furiously at the boys, then ran off and cringed in terror.

The sixth time the vandals tossed a firecracker over the wall, McMullan was working on his car in the back-yard with Anne Marie, his one-year-old daughter. The firecracker landed next to her and hissed. Sparks flew. As Anne Marie bent down to pick it up, Bruno ignored his fear of explosives. He jumped in front of her and grabbed the firecracker with his teeth.

The firecracker blew up with such force that it threw Bruno onto his back. Trembling, he lay on the ground, his four paws stiff in the air. His blood was splattered all around. Smoke billowed from his mouth, which was a bloody pulp. Half his jaw was blown away.

Certain that Bruno was dead, McMullan rushed over to him. But the dog was still breathing, though obviously suffering from hideous pain. McMullan scooped him up and took him to the veterinarian. Although Bruno was disfigured for life after taking the hit for Anne Marie, the dog survived.

———

ANIMALS DON'T merely shield people. As Bruno did, they often go after the threat, take the hit, and pay a terrible price. Acting with compassion can cost the animals dearly.

When seventy-nine-year-old Lillian Woodside was sweeping leaves in front of her Buffalo, New York, home, an eighty-pound Akita broke through its fence next door, barked at the woman, and bit her. Screaming, she tried to defend herself, but the Akita kept attacking—until Oliver, a tiny, twelve-pound Yorkshire terrier who lived in the neighborhood, heard the fight and dashed over to help her. When Oliver charged the Akita, it chomped into him as if he were a dog biscuit. But Oliver kept up his defense until two neighbors drove by, broke up the fight, and took the woman to a hospital. Oliver's injuries required nine stitches; he had risked his life for a woman he barely knew.

• One Easter morning in Scranton, Iowa, farmhand Richard Meiner swung open the door of a farrowing house to let the sows out of their crates for exercise.

Beside him was Buddy, a five-month-old basset hound who belonged to Meiner's boss. The puppy was as startled as Meiner was when the door accidentally hit a five-hundred-pound sow who'd somehow escaped from her crate. She'd recently given birth to a litter of piglets and now was intent on protecting them—and getting Meiner out of the farrowing house.

The sow snorted with anger, lowered her head, and lunged at him. She sank her teeth into his knee. Meiner yelled in pain, but his boss was not around to hear his cries. Buddy came to the rescue instead. The puppy ran, barking, at the sow.

The sow rooted her snout, her most powerful weapon, under Buddy's little body and flipped him with a quarter-ton of force against the wall. Despite his pain, Buddy kept yowling and fighting her long enough for Meiner to run out of the farrowing house and find his boss's father. Together, they corralled the sow back into her crate.

They rushed Buddy to the vet, who set the pup's broken leg. For the rest of his life Buddy limped, the price he paid for protecting Meiner and taking the brunt of the sow's fury.

• Chelsea, a golden retriever, sat at Chris Dittmar's feet one evening while he talked with his neighbors, Bill and Jeannie Ridlehuber, in front of their Houston homes. Four thugs drove up, got out of their car, and sauntered up and down the driveways on the block.

"Know what time it is?" one of them asked Dittmar.

The question made his skin crawl. With a premonition that he was about to be mugged, he whispered to Jeannie to go inside her house and call the police.

The hooligans walked away, then turned around and came back. Two of them aimed loaded pistols at Dittmar's and Ridlehuber's temples.

"Get in the street," one of the gunmen demanded.

Before anyone could move, Chelsea bared her teeth and snarled. She jumped on one of the gunmen and snapped at his throat. He was so frightened of her that he shifted his aim from Dittmar to the dog—and shot her. Blood spurted from her shoulder, but she kept fighting.

Ridlehuber and Dittmar ran for their lives into his garage. The gunmen fired four more times at Chelsea— instead of at the fleeing men—and then escaped in their car. Chelsea limped into the shadows. All alone, she had no one on the street to help her.

Desperate to find her, Dittmar loaded a shotgun and searched the neighborhood. With apprehension knotting his stomach, he steeled himself for finding her dead.

Two blocks away, he saw her, hiding. "Chelsea!" he shouted, relieved.

Chelsea hobbled toward him and rested her head on his knee. Blood seeped through her fur. A .38-caliber slug had barely missed bones and organs and had lodged along her chest wall. Eventually, she recovered from the shots that were meant to kill people she loved.

WHEN LISA Funderburk gave birth to Lyndsey, her daughter, she worried that her dachshund-beagle mutt Klutz would be jealous. She needn't have worried. Klutz became even more fiercely devoted to Lyndsey than he was to Lisa, even though he'd lived with Lisa for the past eight years.

If Lyndsey wailed in her crib, Klutz ran to Lisa, bit her pant leg, and tugged her to the baby. If Lisa did not respond immediately, the dog ran in circles around her and barked. Klutz was just as protective when Lyndsey tried to crawl up the stairs; he grabbed her by the seat of her pants and pulled her back to safety. Lyndsey, he clearly felt, was his personal charge.

Just before Christmas, when the child was three years old, she got up from the kitchen table in Lehigh Acres, Florida. "I'm going to let Klutzie in," she said.

She opened the door to the backyard and called Klutz, but he did not heave himself up from his daily sunning spot in the grass as he normally would. Nor did he waddle on his short little legs across the threshold. Lyndsey started out the door to get him but suddenly stopped when he jumped up, barking and yapping at her.

Klutz continued to bark, and his paws thudded against the ground again and again, as if he were jumping on something. Neither Lisa nor her parents got up from the table to check on him until his barks turned suddenly to shrieks, then to piercing, angry yelps. Lisa ran to the door, pushed Lyndsey aside, and heard a rattling sound, as if someone were shaking dice in a tin can.

A rattlesnake was coiled under a bush and ready to strike.

"Get back!" Lisa screamed at Klutz.

It was too late. The dog stopped yelping and collapsed on the ground. But he still seemed determined to protect Lyndsey from the snake. He lurched to his feet and staggered toward it, then fell to his stomach. He raised himself up again and crawled toward the snake. Once more the rattler struck.

Lisa froze. Her heart seemed to stop beating. She couldn't watch her beloved dog die before her eyes without trying to save him.

She grabbed her car keys. To keep from passing the snake to reach Klutz, she ran out the front door and around the house to the back, where Klutz lay foaming at the mouth. Though he was unable to stand, he wouldn't give up. He still flailed his paws at the snake and tried to fight it.

Lisa picked up the dog, rushed to her car, and lay him on the seat beside her. As she sped two miles to the nearest veterinary clinic, she begged Klutz, "Don't die! Please, don't die!" Christmas was coming, she reminded him. "You have to open your presents. I've bought you a new bed and a squeaky toy. Don't die!"

Klutz, scarcely able to breathe, trembled violently. His eyes rolled back in his head, and he went into convulsions.

How could she help him? Whenever *she* was sick, Klutz always climbed on her and refused to leave until she felt better. He was so emotionally connected to her that once he'd even known that she was delirious when she was miles from home in an emergency room. At just the moment she'd called his name in the hospital, he had "heard" her at home and scratched her bedroom door so fiercely that his paws bled. What could she possibly do now to repay him for his devotion?

In the clinic, Dr. Darry Griebel set Klutz on a steel table and examined him. The snake had bitten him twice, on his eyelid and in his eyeball. Griebel measured four inches between each fang mark.

As a snake grows older and larger, its fangs get farther apart, he told Lisa. "That snake had to be huge. At least five feet."

The bigger the snake, the more venom it has in its bite, he explained. And the older the dog, the less strength it has to fight for its life. At age eleven, Klutz was at a great disadvantage.

"I'm not sure we ought to try and save him," Griebel said sadly.

"We *have* to try," Lisa argued. "Do anything you can. I don't care how much it costs."

Griebel gave Klutz intravenous antibiotics and two shots of antivenin, then put him in a cage to keep a careful watch on him.

"The first forty-eight hours will be the most dangerous," he warned. "If he doesn't die in two days, he'll probably make it."

Lisa loved Klutz so much that she was not sure *she* would make it. Two days would seem like two years. She sat beside his cage with tears rolling down her face and remembered all the times when he had licked them off her cheeks.

"You can't die this way," she told Klutz again and again. "I couldn't stand it if you died trying to save Lyndsey."

Klutz tried to turn his head to lick her hand but couldn't. His head and neck had swollen to the size of a St. Bernard's; his whole body had ballooned out of shape. He closed his eyes and retreated into himself, miles away in a world of pain.

Lisa got up to leave, so he could rest. "You have to make it," she whispered. "You have to come home."

She returned to her house for her mother's credit card to pay Griebel (and she learned that her father had killed the snake with a shovel). On her way back to the clinic, she bought Klutz a teddy bear and hung a medal with a heart and two praying hands around his neck. When she put the bear in the cage beside Klutz, he opened his eyes and tried to scoot closer to her—but he could not move. He whimpered. Tears wet Lisa's cheeks.

The next day she returned with special meals that her mother had cooked and packed in plastic containers: spaghetti and meatballs, browned hamburger and rice, scrambled eggs, and apple pie. For the first time since Klutz had come to the clinic, he ate—not voraciously, but with interest. The first twenty-four of his forty-eight hours of danger had passed.

The next twenty-four hours were also uneventful. Klutz seemed to be winning his fight for survival. His swelling went down enough that he could sit on his plump little haunches or stand with his stomach hanging, as always, just inches from the ground. He held out his paws to Lisa.

She patted him. "You're such a wonderful dog."

Though he appeared much better, she did not bring Lyndsey to visit him for a few days. Lisa worried that his puffy face and weakness might upset her daughter. But by Christmas Eve, he seemed to have improved so much that the doctor said Klutz could go home. Alert and eager, he trotted across the clinic's grass to Lisa's car.

When the dog got home and first saw Lyndsey, he whined joyfully, wagged his tail, and licked her. Lisa put him on pillows and blankets in a playpen, so Lyndsey could sit outside it and talk to him. Whenever she left the room, Klutz, unable to follow, cried so plaintively that she hurried back. She sang to him and chattered about Christmas.

Just before midnight, the family left for mass to thank God that Klutz seemed to be recovering. When they got home, however, he was sick again. He was panting, scarcely able to breathe. His heart was beating harder than normal, and his eyes were glazed. For the rest of the night, Lisa stayed with him, patted him, and prayed for him.

On Christmas morning she called Griebel. "Klutz doesn't look so good." The lump in her throat felt like a boulder.

"Bring him to my office. I'll meet you there."

Lisa was amazed that even on Christmas, Griebel was willing to leave his family in order to help Klutz. He picked up the dog and laid him on the examination table.

"He's having complications from the antivenin," Griebel determined. "He needs a blood transfusion."

After that, nothing more could be done for him, except to wait and see what happened.

The waiting was agony for Lisa, Lyndsey, Lisa's parents, and Griebel. At four o'clock the next morning, Klutz died.

At six o'clock, Griebel, who had not left Klutz for nearly twenty-four hours, called Lisa and told her Klutz was gone. "He gave his life for Lyndsey," he said.

Lyndsey weighed twenty-eight pounds, exactly Klutz's weight. Getting her to the hospital—five miles farther away than Griebel's clinic—in time to save her life would have been impossible. If she'd been bitten, she would have died. Klutz had attacked the snake, so she would live.

Klutz had also fought to stay alive as long as he could for Lyndsey's sake. "He must have been determined to go back home and make sure she was all right," Griebel told Lisa. "Once he knew that, then he could die."

Klutz had died knowing that he'd succeeded in protecting Lyndsey.

CHAPTER TEN

NATURAL HEALERS

FLORENCE NIGHTINGALE said, "A small pet is an excellent companion for the sick." The benefits that she intuitively recognized have now been proven by medical studies. The mere presence of an animal, for example, lowers not only people's anxiety, but also their blood pressure, heart rate, and even cholesterol. Studies have also shown that pet owners, in comparison with people who have no animals at home, visit doctors significantly fewer times annually and are more likely to survive the year after being released from a coronary-care unit.

All the studies underscore what many people have always believed: Animals can sometimes actually heal physical illness. They do it by sensing that something is wrong, then trying to help. Their compassion is good medicine.

• In *Alert* magazine, Andrea Leigh Ptak gives an example of this medicine. Emma, a Lhasa apso, belonged to a woman who had tried everything her doctor recommended to cure her migraine headaches. Nothing had worked. When Emma jumped onto the woman's lap to be petted, however, the woman's headaches grew less painful and intense—and sometimes even disappeared. The doctor's explanation: Emma's body, by warming the woman's hands, drew blood away from her brain and lessened vascular flooding *and* pain. Just as important, Emma offered emotional comfort and soothed her. Whenever the woman went to a place where bright lights might set off a migraine, she usually brought along Emma, her living, breathing headache remedy.

• Handsome, a fluffy Persian cat, was brought to live in a nursing home as a companion to Marie, who was lonely and depressed. She dealt with her emotions by curling up into a fetal position and refusing to talk with anyone. She also constantly scratched at sores on her legs. Handsome apparently wanted to make her healthy. Every time she scratched her legs, he jumped on her hands to force her to stop. In a few weeks, her sores were gone—and so were Marie's depression and withdrawal. Now, whenever anyone would listen, she would not stop talking about her cat.

• Alpha, an orange tabby mentioned in *Cat Fancy* magazine, seemed concerned that his person woke one night with a stomach ache. When she sat up in bed, he left his sleeping spot and pressed himself against her.

She told him that her stomach hurt; Alpha acted as if he understood. Looking up at her with caring orange eyes, he purred and touched her stomach exactly where the pain was. Somehow, the soft patting of his paw made her feel better. When she lay down again, her stomach ache was gone.

MICKEY NIEGO had asthma attacks and migraine headaches so excruciating that she quit her job in Manhattan and withdrew emotionally; she felt sick all the time. A friend gave her Jake, a bullmastiff puppy, to cheer her through her illness. Instead of boosting her morale, though, *he* became even sicker than Niego was. She nursed him through pneumonia, parvo virus, and distemper.

When he got well, their roles reversed, said Niego, and Jake became "the best possible parent" and healer.

On shopping trips, which she hated and usually avoided, he trotted along beside her and seemed to be waiting for one of her asthmatic coughs. When she did begin to cough, he leaned against her and made her slow down and breathe in his rhythm, as she rested her hand on his neck. Just touching his fur, she said, was like "closing a circuit and making me grounded." The asthma went away.

Months later she felt strong enough to take a job at Manhattan's A.S.P.C.A., but she dreaded the headaches that she always got on commutes. As she drove into the city, Jake, lying in the bucket seat next to her, rested his head on her lap. His slow, reassuring breaths were "like relaxing ocean waves," Niego said. She stroked his head and absorbed his calm. The migraines went away.

Her job required her to do occasional live television interviews. As she prepared for the first one, her stomach churned with the anxiety that, in the past, had made her sick. Jake butted his head against her—a sign, she thought, of his insistence that she push ahead and sail through the interview. Friendly and eager, he faced the cameras with her. When she became nervous, he looked at her with sympathetic, encouraging eyes. The churning stomach went away.

One day Niego realized that she had not taken her asthma medication for months. Her headaches, too, had dwindled down to infrequent minor episodes; then they had just disappeared.

"Jake's eyes told me, 'I love you. I'll never let anything happen to you,'" she said. "His presence was like big strong arms that hugged and protected me."

Jake's comforting presence had healed her.

———

WHEN JOAN PRICE was driving along a road near her house in Sebastopol, California, another car crashed, head on, into her. One of her legs was severely fractured; her foot was nearly broken off. After ten days in the hospital, she came home depressed, angry, and still haunted by the experience. At night she had recurring nightmares about the accident. During the day, even when she took prescription drugs, she was in constant pain.

"My leg feels as if brambles are being burned into it," she told her friends.

Her friends checked up on her and brought her food because she lived alone. And her gold-eyed cat, Ylla, a little independent puffball, also aided her recovery—even though, before the accident, the cat had always refused to sit in Price's lap or sleep on her bed.

Ylla had previously lived with a man who had no respect or love for cats. He had let his dog gnaw on her and had thrown her against the door when she'd tried to cuddle up to him. To get rid of her, once and for all, he'd brought her to Price's next door neighbor.

"You have to take her," he'd insisted. "If I keep her, I'll kill her."

When the cat wandered over to Price's deck and looked up at her with desperate eyes, Price knew she had to rescue her. Price brought her in the house.

Though Ylla was extremely loving, she had always kept her distance. Until the accident, that is. When Price came home from the hospital, the cat jumped on the bed and sniffed her leg, then settled on her chest. All day and night, Ylla assumed a roosting-chicken position on Price and purred nonstop. If Price turned over or shifted her weight, Ylla did, too, to accommodate the change of position. Sticking to Price like a barnacle, she left only occasionally to eat or patrol the yard.

Ylla's constant love and attention kept Price from feeling alone. The cat in her arms also helped her believe that she would recover from her injury. A few weeks after leaving the hospital, Price was able to get out of bed for a short time each day. Then for several months she clumped around on crutches. As Price slowly regained her strength, Ylla hovered over her, reassured her, and healed her with purrs.

"TAKE THE CAT. Take the cat." Michelle's friend thrust an orange-and-white kitten toward her. "It's sick. It's mother must have abandoned it. You can tell it's about to starve to death."

"I don't want it," Michelle said glumly.

"Take it."

"It's too much trouble."

"Then keep it till you can find somebody else to take it. If you don't, it's going to die."

Michelle felt that she was going to die herself. At age twenty-two, she'd been taking drugs and drinking heavily for eight years. She was so sick all the time that her friend had just brought her to a lodge in Woodstock, New York, to make her lie in bed and regain her strength. Her emotional world had also caved in. That fall she'd gone outside and realized that the whole summer had passed without her even noticing it. Ill and crying many times a day, she'd even threatened suicide.

"I don't care about the kitten," she told her friend.

He set it gently on her bed.

Michelle examined the pathetic creature. He was dirty and just as weak and sick as she was. She agreed to keep him only until he got healthy again; then she'd give him away. To stop herself from getting attached, she also refused to name him.

A few days later, Michelle tossed clothes into her suitcase to go back to New York City. The kitten lay in a heap on the bed. On the drive home he seemed so limp and feeble that Michelle and her friend stopped to see a veterinarian.

"He's only got a fifty-fifty chance of living," he said.

The vet gave Michelle a bottle of baby formula to keep the kitten alive until they reached Manhattan. He advised her to take him to a clinic near her home as soon as possible.

She fed the formula to the kitten in the car and steeled herself against caring whether he lived or died. She didn't have the energy to be a kitten's nursemaid, she told herself. This cat would have to make it on his own, or not.

A Manhattan vet treated the kitten with antibiotics. Michelle took him to live in her one-room apartment, fed him out of a bottle, and gradually weaned him to cottage cheese and eggs. He grew attached to her as if she were his mother. The kitten followed her around and seemed to thrive under her care.

Then one of his eyes developed a runny discharge. Michelle brought him back to the vet, who diagnosed a severe infection.

"He has to have this eye removed," he said.

During the surgery, Michelle paced her apartment and worried. She drank vodka and tonics and flipped through ancient magazines. The next day when she brought the one-eyed kitten home, she named him Cyclops. Later she shortened the name to Clopsy and admitted to herself that she could never give the kitten away. He was hers, for keeps.

As Michelle lay in bed and tried to gather the energy to stop drinking, get well, and turn her life around, Clopsy snuggled up in her arms and suckled on her sweat shirt. Every day he covered the front of whatever she was wearing with a big, drooly spot. Week after week, her clothes hamper piled up with blouses, pajama tops, and turtlenecks that were damp from Clopsy's nursing on the fabric.

The kitten clearly needed her. Slowly, day by day, Clopsy became Michelle's reason to clean up her act.

"Come home. Live with me," Michelle's mother offered. "I'll watch after you. You can go to detox."

"I'm scared."

Michelle finally agreed, and she and Clopsy moved in with her mother. For the next several months Michelle went through detox and rehab, then started attending Alcoholics Anonymous meetings. Her long winter of substance abuse slowly thawed to a spring of better health.

Her healing was not without occasional setbacks, though. Michelle was constantly sick and often spent entire days in bed. She was also frequently so depressed and frightened that she closed her bedroom door and refused to speak to anyone. No matter how she behaved, Clopsy loyally stayed in bed with her.

If she went anywhere at all, to the bathroom or the kitchen, he followed her. He seemed to be trying to show her how important she was to him. Instead of just receiving care, he was giving it back, and his presence brought her peace of mind.

When Michelle was finally sober and physically strong, she and Clopsy moved into their own apartment. She found a job and, years later, also met a man who became her husband. All of the positive changes had occurred, she told him, because of her orange-and-white cat.

"He taught me that I was capable of caring for something," she said.

Now a bruiser of a tomcat, Clopsy still curls up like a baby in Michelle's arms and nurses on her shirts. But he's not only suckling *her;* the "nourishing" is mutual.

"I can always turn to him," Michelle says. "He loves me unconditionally." Clopsy repaid Michelle for nurturing him as a fragile kitten by becoming her healer as well.

CHAPTER ELEVEN

STANDING *in* HARM'S WAY

CHERYL ESSEX'S husband was out of town on a business trip. She sat down in her kitchen late one evening and phoned a friend. While they chatted, her silver schnauzer-terrier mutt Rosie scrambled to the condo's balcony door. Looking pensive, she pressed her little black nose against the glass and barked.

"Hush, Rosie." Cheryl went back to her phone conversation.

Rosie would not hush. She dashed to the condo's front door and barked again. When Essex continued to ignore her, Rosie came into the kitchen and barked directly at her as if she were telling her in no uncertain terms to pay attention. Essex still refused to hang up the phone.

Rosie then became exceedingly upset, darting back and forth from the balcony to the front door. When Essex kept talking to her friend, Rosie stopped her usual high-pitched barks and growled deep, throaty growls. Her fur stood on end.

"I've got to call you back. Something must be wrong," Essex told her friend. "Either Rosie's sick or something's happening down in the garage."

Yet Rosie did not look the least bit sick. With the windows closed and the air conditioner humming, she also had no way of knowing what was going on downstairs. Still, since the police had arrested four hoodlums for breaking into cars in the garage two nights earlier, Essex was worried about her own car. She decided to go downstairs and check it.

The instant Essex opened her front door, Rosie tore down all three flights of stairs as if she had urgent business to attend to. She waited, growling, on the bottom step until Essex reached her. Then Rosie became protective. She yowled at a rustling noise in the trees nearby, dashed toward them, and disappeared into the dark. Essex smelled gasoline fumes and ran to her car. Someone had broken into it and had tried to steal the radio. A gasoline-filled milk jug sat on the pavement in a large puddle of gas.

As Rosie dashed back to the garage, Essex realized that someone had intended to burn the condo's three buildings. She also realized that her dog had been desperately trying to keep her safe. Essex scooped up Rosie, hurried upstairs, and called the police. With the dog still in her arms, Essex and a neighbor banged on people's doors and woke all the other residents. As they gathered in the garage, a neighbor showed Essex towels that had been soaked in gasoline and packed around the stairs.

Police theorized that the gang had come back to retaliate for their four members being arrested two nights before. A single lighted match to the gasoline-soaked towels would have torched the condo's buildings and trapped the residents, many of whom were elderly, in flames. Although police never arrested the arsonists, at least Rosie had caught them in the act and scared them off, saving 120 lives.

THOUGH DOGS are expected to bark at arsonists, burglars, and intruders, no one expects cats to warn anyone of impending crime. And yet they do. Like dogs, cats can be extremely protective of the people they are emotionally bonded to.

• In *Cat Fancy*, David Blume described a couple who noticed that their calico cat was leaping from one window to the next in their bedroom one evening. Although, at the time, they did not try to figure out why she seemed so upset, the next morning they wished they'd paid attention. Someone had stolen the battery from their car.

• Blume also related the story of an elderly woman who heard a knock on the door one night. As she turned on the porch light to answer the door, her cat, Tug, acted strangely. Tug jumped onto a chair by the door, hunched down on his stomach, and flattened his ears. His fur rose like needles along his back.

The elderly woman opened the door to see a young woman standing there. She asked to use the telephone to call for help because her car had broken down.

The elderly woman glanced at Tug, who looked as if he were about to spring on an enemy and claw it to death. She decided not to let in the stranger and told her that she had no telephone. She shut and locked the door.

The next day she learned that two men had been hiding beside her house when the woman had knocked. A few hours after they left, another senior citizen about a mile away had been murdered. Tug's elderly owner called the police, and a week later they arrested the young woman and her two male companions. All of them later confessed to the murder.

• Lauren MacLaren slept soundly while her black-and-gold calico named Cali perched as usual on the windowsill. She had been rescued as an abused kitten from the pound in Toronto. The cat stared out into the night and observed a man at the end of the driveway sneak past MacLaren's bedroom window and up her porch stairs.

Cali pricked her ears. She knew that something was wrong. When the man turned the knob of the door to the house, she leaped on MacLaren's bed and cried. The cat jumped on her again and again until MacLaren opened her eyes and heard the intruder rattling the door, about to break in.

Her heart in her throat, MacLaren watched the doorknob turn in the moonlight. To prevent the man from knowing she was awake, she crawled to a phone in another room and called the police, who arrested him on her back porch. Cali went back to her guard post on the windowsill.

ANIMALS DO more than just warn of impending crime. They often jump right in and defend people they care about from muggers, rapists, and murderers. What is so astounding about their defense is the creatures' willingness to take on impossible opponents and be brutalized by them. The animals' concern wins out over their instinct for self-preservation.

• Tinkerbelle, a thirteen-pound mutt in Indianapolis, was watching over ten-year-old Tim Dawson, who was sick and staying home from school. When a man broke into the house, tiny Tinkerbelle grabbed the intruder's pant leg with her teeth, leaped on him, and bit his hand. Her ferocity sent him running.

• One night, Meatball, a German shepherd, followed Mrs. Robert Keith into her greenhouse in Morris, Alabama. After she'd been talking with her mother on the telephone, Keith had heard the quiet click of someone picking up her phone's extension there. Keith and Meatball found a man. The dog lunged at him and chased him to his car. Before the burglar could close the door, Meatball bit his leg and hung on—even when the man put his car in gear and sped away. As the car dragged Meatball along the road, the asphalt cracked his toenails and bruised his paw pads, but he persevered in protecting Keith.

• Brandy, a springer spaniel puppy, attacked a teenage burglar who had broken into her Tucson, Arizona home. The teenager shot the woman who lived there, then turned on Brandy and shot the dog in the chest, jaw, belly, and legs. Weak from loss of blood and in excruciating pain, the puppy was still determined to save the woman. Brandy chased the burglar out of the house, where police shot and killed him. The dog's wounds gradually healed.

OSKAR, a Chesapeake Bay retriever, was a supremely social dog. From the age of seven weeks, he sailed on boats, rode up ski slopes on chair lifts, and slept through dinner parties at Chris Eschenberg's feet. Yipping with joy, Oskar also pounced on Eschenberg's friends and made them *his* friends. He seemed sure that all people were good.

Of course, to Oskar, Eschenberg was the best person of all. The minute Eschenberg pulled into his New Orleans garage, Oskar whined and barked to urge him to hurry into the house. Once Eschenberg walked through the front door, Oskar leaped on him and whined and barked again with pleasure. The greetings were routine.

So routine that Eschenberg was instantly worried when he came home one night and his house was quiet. He got out of the car and walked down the narrow path to the front door. Instead of Oskar's whining and barking, someone rustled and mumbled under the house. Most likely a homeless person had settled in for the night, Eschenberg thought in distress; but the night was too dark to see anything. Eschenberg hurried toward his door.

A man crawled out and pointed a gun at him.

"Hey, man, get on in that house," he ordered.

The man seemed nervous and frail. Eschenberg, a doctor, assumed he was on crack. Eschenberg also assumed that he was about to undergo his *third* robbery in just a few months. But this time would be worse than the others—instead of merely taking Eschenberg's wallet and running, this man was coming into the house.

Oskar would be waiting at the door to begin his ecstatic welcome. As soon as Eschenberg turned the key in his lock, the dog would yelp with joy, as thrilled to see the robber as he was any of Eschenberg's friends. The robber, however, would be terrified and would shoot Oskar. Opening the door would be his death sentence.

Eschenberg had no choice; the man was pointing a gun at him and telling him to go inside. With adrenaline coursing through him, Eschenberg unlocked the door and pushed it open a few inches. Oskar was silent, nowhere in sight. Eschenberg opened the door farther. Still no trace of his dog.

Nearly sick with worry, Eschenberg stepped over the threshold. The robber followed. Oskar, without a sound of warning, leaped on the man, bit his arm, and shook it violently. The robber, screaming, jerked his arm away and hit Eschenberg on the side of the head—then climbed the fence and ran away.

Eschenberg turned on the entry light. Oskar was standing in a pool of blood. Blood was smeared all over his face, chest, legs, and paws.

"He shot you!" Still more adrenaline flowing through him, Eschenberg bent down to examine his dog but found no wounds.

Oskar was covered not with his own blood, but with the robber's. This dog obviously could tell the difference between friend and enemy.

A THREE-HUNDRED-POUND pig, raised from a tiny piglet by Rick Charles, lived in his chain-link-fenced backyard near Houston and was a gentle, docile member of the family. During the day, the pig rooted around in mud and played with Charles's children; at night she slept in a giant pile of leaves.

One morning four burglars, rampaging through the neighborhood, knocked at doors and, if no one answered, kicked them in and robbed the houses. By noon the men had loaded their stolen pickup truck with furniture, jewelry, coin collections, and video and stereo equipment.

The burglars took off down the street so rapidly that a Houston policeman picked up the truck on radar and chased it to give the driver a ticket. The robbers assumed that he was after them because of their booty and the stolen truck, not because of their speed. Eager to escape, the driver went faster—and broadsided another car.

The squealing of brakes and crunch of fenders could not stop the four burglars. They jumped from the truck and took off on foot. The policeman, who'd been chasing them, radioed for help. Soon twenty officers arrived and swarmed the neighborhood.

One of the burglars found a hiding place under a house near where Charles's pig was rooting in the mud. When the police closed in on the robber, he ran to her backyard and clambered over the chain-link fence. At best, he intended to hide in her leaf pile. At worst, he was going to break into Charles's house, take hostages, and make a getaway in their car.

Whatever the robber's plan, the pig would have none of it. Protective of her human family, she charged, threw her heft against the man, and bit his leg. Blood spewed from the bite. When he screamed and tried to run away, she knocked him to the ground, pinned him there, and stared him down with a threatening expression. Until the police arrived, she warmed the stubble on the robber's cheeks with her moist breath and refused to let him move.

DONALD MORGAN, a retired policeman, pretended to slap his wife, Pat. She pretended to be in horrible pain; she screamed an agonizing, desperate scream and "tried" to shove away her husband.

Their German shepherd Yogi heard the "attack" and came running. Growling and baring his teeth, he made his point: Donald had better stop the slapping. When he didn't, Yogi pulled his arm and nipped his hand. When that didn't stop him, Yogi jumped on Donald and let him know that he was about to go after him in earnest.

"I wonder what would happen if a man actually attacked me?" Pat asked Donald after one of these training sessions. "Do you think Yogi would really fight someone off?"

"I don't know," Donald answered.

He and Pat hoped they would never have to find out.

When Donald died, Pat continued living with Yogi in an isolated lake house near Abilene, Texas. One night after getting ready for bed, she put Yogi in his fenced pen and started back toward her bedroom. Suddenly she heard someone at the front door. Since it was locked, she figured she'd have plenty of time to bring Yogi back into the house if she needed protection. She picked up her portable phone to call the police if necessary and went to the door to see who was there. A man was standing in her living room.

Pat was so alarmed that she dropped the phone while dialing "0." She ran toward the back door to get

Yogi, but the man stopped her. Without a word, he slammed his fist into her face so hard that she reeled back into her bedroom.

Sprawled on the floor, she told herself, "I'm going to die. Donald died last year, and now it's my turn."

Yogi was her only chance to live. Fenced in his pen, he would have to use all his strength to get to her—if he *could* get to her at all. As she screamed for Yogi, the man fell on her and hit her again and again. He yanked at her pajama top and tried to rip it off. Pat kicked, clawed, and yelled.

"Yogi! Yogi!"

"Hello? Hello? Hello!!" The operator's voice from the phone on the floor punctuated Pat's shouts.

The man beat her into silence. He wrapped a pair of panty hose around her neck and choked her. With no oxygen, she grew weak and faint. When she tried to call Yogi one last time, the man put a knife to her throat and cut into her. Blood trickled down her neck.

Outside, Yogi heard Pat's call. He leaped over his chain-link fence and barreled toward the house. He then threw himself through a screen door onto the porch. When a heavy metal storm door blocked his way into the kitchen, he backed up and hurled himself against the metal again and again until it caved in and the locks broke.

Yogi tore into the bedroom. He growled, barked, and leaped on all fours onto the man. As the man kicked him away, Yogi yelped in pain but continued his attack. The power of the dog's body knocked the man off Pat.

Jumping up, he tried to escape, but Yogi bit his leg and kept his teeth clamped into it.

Pat, knowing she was safe now that Yogi was there, lost consciousness. When she came to, her dog was still trying to protect her by growling and barking—but this time, at the police. The telephone operator had heard Pat scream and notified them.

"Mrs. Morgan. Mrs. Morgan," one of the policemen shouted from the window. "Your dog won't let us in to help you."

Yogi stood over Pat and growled ferociously.

She managed to take hold of his collar. "It's okay, Yogi," she whispered. "These are the good guys. Let them in."

Since Yogi had grown up seeing Donald and his colleagues in policemen's uniforms, he quickly realized that the men were friends when they came inside. He stood by and let them take care of Pat. Around the house, they found pieces of blood-soaked cloth, which Yogi had ripped from the assailant's pants and shirt.

That day Yogi proved that he was capable of defending Pat in a real attack. Although the assailant was never caught, Yogi was ready for him if he returned. But he never came back.

CHAPTER TWELVE

CONCERN *in the* COLD

LATE ON a winter night, Indian Red, a Morgan–quarter horse mix, walked along a deserted country road in Ontario, Canada. He stopped, raked his hoof in the snow, and peered at the ground intensely. The temperature was dropping, and he should have looked for shelter, but he didn't. In the wind and cold, he stayed beside the road.

When occasional cars passed and shined their headlights on him, he neighed and whinnied. But the drivers ignored him and drove by. He waited patiently for another chance to attract attention until, finally, someone did stop to see if anything was wrong.

Why would a horse be shivering and whinnying beside a road so late at night? the driver wondered.

The man climbed out of his car and searched a snow-covered ditch near the horse. A seventy-seven-year-old woman had fallen into the ditch. Since she was unable to crawl up to the road and get help for herself,

Indian Red had been trying in every way possible to get it for her, even though she was a stranger to him.

Animals, like Indian Red, can be extremely kind to people who need help in snow and ice.

ON AN ICY, fifteen-degree morning in Ontario, Canada, Brian Holmes let Samantha, his Alsatian shepherd, out for her daily patrol of his property. She was a large but graceful dog, rescued from a stable where someone had beaten her. She still cowered at the sight of sticks, but the abuse had not ruined her ability to love.

On agile paws, she made her way through the snow, her breath in clouds around her head, wind ruffling her fur. She stopped, sniffed, and checked Holmes's driveway for pawprints and other messages. In the rural landscape all was quiet. The weather was sullen and gray.

Half a mile away, three-year-old Donald Johnston climbed out of bed and looked through the house for his father, Darryl. The man was sleeping on the sofa with good reason to be tired: The night before, his wife had given birth to Donald's sister. Darryl had been up with them till daylight.

As Donald roamed the house, he felt so lonely for his mother that he decided to go and see her at the hospital thirty miles away. Wearing just sweat pants, a t-shirt, and a light, unbuttoned jacket, he rolled his yellow, battery-operated riding car out of the house and started down the road.

Snow was piled high along the sides. A blustery wind shook the trees. In such an isolated rural area, no drivers passed by. All alone, Donald pushed his car for half a mile.

When he stopped to rest, he knew he was lost; and now he was scared. He had no idea which way to turn to find his mother *or* his father. He was shivering uncontrollably, and his hands were numb. He could not make his icy feet keep moving.

Back home on the sofa, Darryl opened his eyes. Something was wrong; the house was too quiet. He got up, went to Donald's room, and found his empty bed. Searching the rest of the house, he did not find his son. Darryl ran outside without bothering to put on his coat.

"Donald!? Donald?" Darryl cupped his hand around his mouth to shout.

All he heard was wind whistling through the trees. Nearly panicking, he ran down the road to look for his son.

So far from home, Donald leaned against his yellow car and cried. He was sure he was all alone, but he was wrong. From the top of a nearby driveway, Samantha watched him on the road and heard his sobs. Concerned, she bounded down to him and began nuzzling him and licking his tears. He wrapped his arms around her and clung to her as she slowly led him up the driveway to her house and to Brian Holmes.

Holmes was working on his computer when he heard his other dog, Monty, bark in the garage. Holmes got up, put on heavy shoes, and walked outside to see if a car was coming up his driveway. Instead of a car, Samantha was carefully making her way toward him with a pathetic little boy hanging onto her. He was wearing no hat; his snow-boot laces were untied; his mittens hung around his neck on strings.

Who on earth was this child that Samantha was bringing home? Holmes asked himself in shock. He and his wife had no immediate neighbors. Only one house in the area had children living there at all. This boy stumbling along beside Samantha was not one of them.

Holmes walked across the driveway toward him. "Are you all right?"

The boy was too cold and frightened to speak. As Samantha licked his face again, he held onto her the way someone hanging from a cliff clings to a rope. The dog kept a watchful eye on him.

Holmes squatted down next to him. "What's your name?"

This time the child answered with chattering teeth.

"Well, then," Holmes said. "Come inside and get warm."

In front of the fireplace, the little boy huddled with Samantha and Monty, who had followed them into the house.

"Can you tell me your name?" Holmes tried again.

". . . Nolal . . . ommiee."

At least, that was a start.

Holmes wanted to look down on the road for the child's parents. "I'm going to leave for a minute," he said. "Samantha will stay here with you."

Instead of bolting toward the door as she always did at the first sign that Holmes was going out, Samantha did not budge from her place beside the boy. She stood guard over him as Holmes hurried to see if the child's parents had had an auto accident or were changing a flat tire on the road. Perhaps, he told himself, they were stuck in a ditch or a snowdrift.

But all he found was a yellow, battery-operated riding car in the middle of the road. Puzzled, he set it at the bottom of his driveway, so that someone searching for the child would see the car and know he was with Holmes. Then he went back to his house and offered cookies to the boy. Samantha hovered over him.

"Can you talk now?" Holmes coaxed. "Can you tell me your name?"

"Donald," he mumbled.

Holmes called his wife, Michelle, who was in town on business. "Do we know anyone with a little boy named Donald?"

"No."

Holmes explained Samantha's rescue. "I don't know where he came from."

"You'd better call the police," Michelle advised.

Holmes contacted the Ontario Provincial Police. Someone, the dispatcher promised, would be at the house in twenty minutes. In the meantime, Holmes made Samantha stay inside—though she was reluctant to give up her charge—and put Donald in his pickup. If he parked on the road, he figured, Donald's parents might pass by and see him.

As Holmes pulled out of his driveway, a neighboring farmer drove up with Darryl, whom he had found walking along in only pants and a shirt, shouting for Donald. When Holmes put Donald in Darryl's arms, he was so grateful to have found his son that he could not speak. Tears misted his eyes. Donald had been missing for an hour and a half, and Darryl had been terrified that he was dead.

Samantha, still back at the house, did not hear Darryl's thanks or see his reunion with his son. Nor did she see relief smooth the worry lines on Darryl's forehead. But her job was over, and she had done it well. For an hour, she'd been supremely loving toward a desperate child.

ONE FEBRUARY afternoon, Jim Gilchrist went for a walk with his rottweiler, Tara, and his golden retriever, Tiree. As they usually did in the winter, they trudged along the frozen shore of Canada's Lake Simcoe. For a while, the walk was pleasant and invigorating. The dogs bounded through the snow as nimbly as huskies.

But then more snow began to fall, and a freezing wind blustered across the lake. Gilchrist decided to turn back toward home. To get there without having to slog through snow banks, he called Tara and Tiree and led them four hundred yards offshore to walk on the lake's ice. The snow became a near-blizzard; and as Gilchrist plowed on, he could see only a short distance in front of him. Snow clung to his eyelashes, blanketed his shoulders, and whitened the dogs' coats.

As Gilchrist hurried along, his dogs ran off in different directions to explore the ice. Suddenly, with a loud crack, the ice gave way beneath him, and he slid into the lake. Fighting panic, he grabbed the jagged edge that circled him and tried to pull himself back out; but each time, pieces of ice broke off in his hands, and he fell back in the water.

The ice, he realized, was not nearly strong enough to hold onto while he pulled his two hundred pounds out of the lake. As he thrashed around to keep from sinking in his heavy, sodden clothes, his mind raced with thoughts of death. He'd heard of snowmobile riders who'd fallen through ice on that very lake and had died so quickly that rescuers found them at the bottom with their hands still clenched around their handlebars. Gilchrist would die just as quickly. In such icy water, he gave himself, at most, five minutes to live.

With snow falling so hard, no one on shore would be likely to see that he was in trouble; because he was so far away, no one would be likely to hear him shout for help. And even if someone *could* see or hear him, reaching him in the few minutes before he froze to death would be impossible. If he were going to survive, he could rely only on himself.

Gilchrist dug his nails into the ice and again tried to pull himself out of the water. He broke more pieces of ice away from the edge. As he repeatedly failed to lift himself out, his rottweiler Tara ran to help him. The ice broke under *her*, and she also fell into the water. Along with Gilchrist, she desperately paddled to keep her head above the surface.

Gilchrist managed to lift himself up just enough to look over the ice. When he saw Tiree dashing toward him, even more dread squeezed his heart. Because Tiree was a retriever, she loved the water. She'd surely either jump in to "play" with him and Tara or crack the ice with her weight and fall through before she ever reached them. Either way, all three of them would soon be dead.

Wagging her tail, Tiree ran toward them to join the "fun." But about twelve feet from Gilchrist, she suddenly stopped and crouched on the ice. Realizing that something terrible was happening with Gilchrist and Tara, she whined high-pitched shivery sounds of anxiety. She also seemed to realize her own danger. Lying on her stomach and thrusting out her legs, spread-eagle, she distributed her weight evenly on the ice and kept herself from falling through. Then she belly-crawled, inch by inch, to Gilchrist and Tara.

When she reached them, she did not jump or fall into the water, as Gilchrist had feared, but carefully stayed at the edge of the ice where she could assist them. To stay afloat, Gilchrist reached up and curled his fingers around her collar. She held him steady. As he clung to her, a man shouted in the distance.

"We're coming to help! Hold on! Hold on!"

Gilchrist held onto his life by holding onto Tiree's collar. But he did not have enough time to wait for the man to rescue him.

Gilchrist helped Tara climb on his shoulders. Still holding onto Tiree, he pushed Tara out of the water. As icicles instantly formed on her fur, she scrambled, shivering and traumatized, onto the ice beside Tiree. Surely Tara would run away and save herself, Gilchrist thought.

Yet she stayed with him, even though she was still terrified. She clearly intended to help. Trembling and whimpering, she lay down on her stomach next to Tiree and let Gilchrist grab her collar, too. Then the two dogs dug their claws into the ice and together slowly started backing up—and dragging Gilchrist from the water.

Because he had nothing to push himself up with, he was dead weight, just hanging. But the dogs kept straining and tugging at him as the ice cracked and shattered beneath their paws. Even though they could have fallen back into the water at any moment, they pulled harder and harder until slowly, with exquisite caution, they clawed their way to ice thick enough to support their weight. Then they tugged with all their might and dragged Gilchrist completely out of the lake.

Shaking uncontrollably from cold and fear, he lay facedown on the ice and tried to gather the strength to stand. The dogs, ecstatic that they'd saved him, barked, wagged their tails, and leaped into the air.

"Stop! Stop!" he shouted at them. If they cracked the ice again, all three of them would be plunged back in the water.

The dogs stopped their celebration and stood protectively beside him until the man who'd shouted, "Hold on!" finally reached them. He helped them home, where Gilchrist took a hot bath, and the dogs got warm and dry.

In the next few days, as Gilchrist recovered from his ordeal, he kept mulling over what had happened to him. He began to feel that his nearly dying had special meaning. Without Tara and Tiree, he would be at the bottom of the lake. Surely, he owed the world a favor in return for his survival.

In gratitude for the good fortune of having two brave and loyal dogs, Gilchrist decided to do something not just for them, but for *all* dogs. He opened a boarding kennel, bred golden retrievers, and trained and worked with any dog that was brought to him.

And he told anyone who would listen, "I'm living proof that dogs are man's best friends." He was also living proof of their compassion.

As Gale Coleman got ready for bed one snowy night in Cambridge, Massachusetts, she noticed her porch light flickering and went outside to fix it. Barefooted and wearing only pajamas and a bathrobe, she climbed onto her porch railing and touched the light fixture with wet, icy hands. An electric shock sent her tumbling fifteen feet to the ground.

For a moment, she huddled, stunned, against the fence in the snow. Then she slowly tried to stand and go indoors. A pain, like a knife, stabbed her chest and prevented her from moving. As her hands and brain grew numb and fear settled in beside the pain, she shouted as loudly as she could for half an hour. But no one came to rescue her.

Falling snow would keep piling on her all night, and she would die if someone didn't help her, she thought. But gradually the cold began to mute her terror. Growing too drowsy to be afraid or to help herself, she closed her eyes. Before losing consciousness, she called out again.

No one heard her except Kayla, a Great Dane locked alone in the house next door. She pricked her ears at Coleman's shouts and pawed the back door, but she could not get out. She settled down on her belly, her front paws extended like an Egyptian sphinx, and waited at the door.

Kayla, a sweet and loving creature, had come to live with Randy Foley after he'd had cancer treatments and wanted a dog to combat the gloom in his house. He'd called his friend, a Great Dane breeder.

"This is a miracle!" she said. "I've got the perfect dog for you!"

Just six months old, Kayla weighed only sixty-five pounds, appalling for a Great Dane. Her former owner had beaten her so badly that he'd broken her hindquarter bones and many of her ribs. After someone had taken her away from him, a veterinarian had put her in a body cast.

"You and Kayla would be great medicine for each other," the breeder urged Foley. He needed comfort while recovering from cancer as badly as Kayla needed comfort while her fractures healed.

In the next six months, Foley and Kayla encouraged each other back to health. Though the Great Dane became physically strong and confident, she was still extremely shy. She never barked. Not once. Not even when strangers knocked at Foley's door.

On that freezing winter night, Foley came home and called to Kayla. "Come on. Let's go for a run before the snow gets too deep."

Normally, at the prospect of running, she would have galloped to the front door and panted eagerly. But she stayed at the back door. Still wanting to get out, she scratched it and pressed her nose against the wood.

Her odd behavior baffled Foley; but if she wanted out, he'd let her out. He opened the door. Kayla scrambled to the fence that separated his house from Coleman's and, with huge paws like shovels, dug snow from under the gate. More baffled, Foley followed her and looked over the fence to see if anything were wrong next door. All he could see were deep piles of snow, growing higher and higher in what was becoming a blizzard.

"Come on, Kayla!" Foley started back toward his house. "If we're going to run, we have to hurry."

Kayla, whose greatest pleasure was their evening jog, refused to follow. Not only did she stand there, intransigent, beside the gate; she also barked a loud, deep, determined bark—the first one Foley had ever heard from her. He whirled around and ran back. After so many months, what could possibly have gotten her to break her silence?

Foley looked over the gate again; for the second time, all he could see was a four-foot snow drift.

"Kayla? What's the matter with you?"

When he turned to go back to his house, she let out a long, urgent howl. Whatever was necessary to get his attention, she was willing to do. The howl was all Foley needed to hear. Certain that something was wrong, he pushed snow away from the gate and shoved it open. Kayla dashed to the snow drift in Coleman's yard and dug into it with her Great Dane power.

When Foley caught up with her, he understood at last why she was distressed. A woman's auburn hair, frozen stiff, stuck out of the snow. Foley joined Kayla in the urgent digging until they exposed the woman's blue face, which was covered with a sheet of ice. The woman was Gale Coleman, Foley's neighbor.

"My God, she's dead!" he shouted. But maybe not.

He had to try and revive her; her life depended on him. Still, he had no idea what he was supposed to do to bring her around. He gritted his teeth. Wind blowing in his face dried his forehead's anxious sweat.

Foley rolled the woman on her back; Kayla curled up beside her and warmed her. To keep Coleman's face out of the snow, Foley put her head on the dog's stomach. As he ran back to his house to call for help, Kayla snuggled closer to Coleman. The Great Dane nuzzled and licked her to revive her.

"Have you ever done CPR before?" the emergency dispatcher asked Foley over the phone.

"I've taken a class, but I've never done it for real."

"You're going to do it for real now."

"I'm not sure I can."

"We'll stay on the line and help you."

"I need all the help I can get."

When Foley ran back to Coleman, he found that Kayla had already started CPR. She had removed at least half the ice from Coleman's face and, with great gentleness, was licking more of it off Coleman's nose and mouth, so she could breathe.

All Foley had to do was continue Kayla's ministrations. Over his portable phone, he followed the emergency dispatcher's instructions, did mouth-to-mouth resuscitation, and got Coleman breathing. Then he covered her with comforters until ambulances and fire engines arrived. Paramedics carried her on a stretcher out of the yard.

"Good job," one of them told Foley—but he should have also complimented Kayla.

"In ten more minutes this woman would have frozen to death," another paramedic said.

Coleman had broken two ribs and punctured a lung, she learned in the hospital. She also learned that Foley was not entirely responsible for saving her life; without Kayla's rescue efforts, Coleman would certainly have been dead.

For the next few months when Foley took his dog to the park each afternoon, Coleman sneaked to his front porch and left treats for her canine paramedic: steaks, boneless chicken, turkey breasts, chicken pies, milk bones. Each day the treat was different.

One evening a Chinese-food delivery man arrived at Foley's front door with white cartons from which delicious aromas wafted. "I have food here for Kayla Foley."

The Great Dane gobbled it down.

Every time Coleman saw Kayla, she hugged and kissed her. "I love you. You're just like Lassie."

Foley found Kayla's rescue amazing. "She could have been grudging and angry after being beaten so badly," he told Coleman. "But she's so full of love."

CHAPTER THIRTEEN

BEYOND *the* CALL OF DUTY

SERVICE ANIMALS, carefully trained to meet a person's needs, can often do far more than most people would ever think of asking them. The animals seem to sense a problem and then try their best to solve it. They try to live up to people's demands on them.

In the International Association of Assistant Dog Partners newsletter, Jean Levitt describes Gentleman Cole, her collie.

As Levitt slowly made her way down the boarding ramp onto a plane, Cole, wearing his backpack, gently braced her and helped her keep her balance. They reached a turn on the ramp, where a man stepped forward to shield a woman with his body from the dog.

When his wife was a child, the man explained, she watched attack dogs tear her parents to pieces in Nazi Germany. At night she still had nightmares of her parents' deaths; whenever she saw a dog, she was terrified.

Learning just then that Cole would be on the plane, the woman had panicked and refused to fly with him. But then, impressed by the dog's so carefully helping Levitt on board, she'd decided to go ahead in spite of her misgivings and take the flight.

Levitt sat at the bulkhead. Cole, his nose pointed toward the aisle, nestled at her feet and fell asleep. The frightened woman and her husband took seats at the back of the plane. When she needed to visit the bathroom, her husband escorted her past Cole. She watched the dog fearfully.

After the plane landed, Levitt waited as other passengers got off first. So did the woman and her husband. When the plane was nearly empty, they came to Levitt. The woman told her that Cole had somehow healed her. His exemplary behavior had helped her realize that dogs were not so bad.

"Would you like to touch Cole?" Levitt asked.

The woman lowered her fingers as if she were about to stick them into flames instead of fur. With tears rolling down her face, she rested her hand on Cole's neck. The collie, understanding that much was being asked of him at just that moment, stood as still as granite, so as not to frighten her. The woman leaned toward him and whispered to him. Still, Cole did not blink or wag his tail.

When her husband bent down, though, Cole knew he was free to be himself. He licked the man's face and welcomed him.

The couple thanked Levitt and filed off the plane. A few minutes later, as Levitt and the collie slowly made their way past the crew, one of the pilots, who had witnessed Cole's compassion, saluted him.

———

IN *FETCH THE PAPER,* Toni and Ed Eames wrote about Ed attending the National Federation of the Blind's "Educate Congress Week" with his golden retriever guide dog, Kirby. The dog started limping so badly that Ed flew home a day early to Modesto, California, and took him to a veterinarian. Ed was expecting to receive only pain medication for his dog, not the vet's shattering diagnosis of cancer.

"An aggressive tumor has destroyed most of the ulna bone on Kirby's right front leg," the vet told Ed.

In the next few weeks, Ed took Kirby for a biopsy and consulted other veterinarians about the dog's treatment. There seemed to be no way around their stark, agonizing recommendation to amputate his leg. Ed and his wife, Toni, took the beautiful dog—who guided so gracefully and conscientiously—for the surgery. The trip to the clinic felt like a ride to an execution.

When Kirby returned home, he was afraid to move. He hated stairs. He did not seem to want to maneuver, disabled.

With such an attitude, what kind of guide dog could he ever become again? Ed debated for weeks about whether to try to get Kirby working again or simply to give up on him and keep him at home as a pet.

Students at the University of California at Davis veterinarian school, where Ed lectured one afternoon, insisted that Kirby return to guiding.

"Sheep dogs herd as well on three legs as on four," one student said. "A guide dog would be the same."

Other people were not so optimistic about Kirby's future.

"Any dog with such a severe disability should never be allowed to work," someone told Ed.

He grew depressed just considering Kirby's options. *If the dog's disability means he shouldn't work, then what does that say about me?* Ed asked himself. Should he, just because he was blind, also give up and fade away?

The answer was no. Ed loved Kirby too much not to fight for his dog's chance to guide again, as he was meant to. In the next months, Ed, Toni, and their friends worked with Kirby constantly to rehabilitate him. But he was still hesitant; he lacked confidence. While he was leading Ed around obstacles, Kirby often stopped and sat down for no other reason than being reluctant to go on.

Ed, from his own experience, could easily understand the stress of conquering a disability. He coaxed and cajoled Kirby to get him to keep working. But the coaxing and cajoling could not continue forever, especially when Ed badly needed to be guided; and he knew it.

Finally, he contacted a dog behaviorist for advice.

"You're treating Kirby exactly the way you've taught parents *not* to treat disabled children," he told Ed.

In other words, Ed had been mollycoddling Kirby. When the dog had not moved forward to guide on the first command, Ed had been giving him positive "strokes" of concern that encouraged Kirby's reticence and loss of spunk.

The next day, Ed followed the behaviorist's advice: Carrying his white cane, Ed brought Kirby out on the street in his harness. When they reached an intersection, the dog was too nervous to cross. He sat down at a corner. Ed put down the harness.

"Okay, Kirby." Ed forced himself to sound firm. "I'd rather walk with you. But if you won't guide me, I'll have to make it on my own." Tapping his white cane on the pavement, Ed started across the intersection alone.

On the corner Kirby watched Ed go. The dog was distraught at being left behind but too frightened to move forward. He whimpered and cried as Ed walked on, then barked to call him back—or to gain courage.

By the time Ed reached the center of the intersection, Kirby made up his mind: Guiding Ed was more important than giving into his own fears. Kirby limped to him. Nudging Ed's leg, just as he'd nudged him to guide him for so many years, Kirby led him the rest of the way across the street.

From then on, wherever Ed needed to be guided, Kirby hobbled loyally beside him on three legs.

AT ONE O'CLOCK in the morning in Fresno, California, Esther Warnes heard a muffled "m-r-r-r-r-r." Sunny, a golden retriever–blond Labrador who had just come to live with her the day before, pushed against Warnes's bed and pawed her hand. The woman opened her eyes.

She heard a shuffling of feet in her family room. Someone had broken in her house.

As she lay there, listening to him grope around in the dark, her stomach lurched. She was alone. Muscular sclerosis had left her body so weak that moving was difficult. Though her new dog could open doors, turn on lights, and help her in and out of the wheelchair, Sunny had no training to protect her.

Yet the dog was all that *could* protect her. As footsteps slowly crossed the house in her direction, Warnes gave her new dog a new command.

"Sunny, guard," she whispered.

Barking and snarling, Sunny tore out of the bedroom. The man's footsteps crashed through the house away from her. Warnes's gate squeaked, and tennis shoes slapped the street's pavement. The house was safe again.

Slowly Warnes got into her wheelchair and rolled to the family room. Growling fiercely on the back of the sofa, Sunny was leaning out the window that the man had removed to get inside. She clearly intended to block him from returning. She also clearly intended to carry out Warnes's "guard."

"You're *such* a good girl!" Warnes' stomach was still jolting, queasy from terror.

Sunny backed through the window and came to her. The dog seemed to sense Warnes's fear. Sunny pressed her body against the woman and lay her head on Warnes's shoulder. Warnes wrapped her arms around her and clung to her. "Good girl. Good girl." The words could hardly express Warnes's gratitude.

Because she could not put back the window and secure her house, Warnes was too afraid to sleep. All she could think about was the man breaking in again and harming her. In her bedroom, she sat in her wheelchair and read psalms to calm herself. Sunny laid her head in Warnes's lap in *her* effort to calm the woman.

After an hour, Warnes told herself, "I've got God and Sunny here with me. That man won't come back."

She got into bed and turned off the light. Sunny jumped on the bed beside her. Gently, the dog slid one paw under Warnes's hand and laid the other paw on top of it.

"Oh, Sunny. Thank you," Warnes whispered, astonished that a dog who was only just getting to know her could be so kind.

As the sun rose around six the next morning, Warnes awoke. All night Sunny had not moved a fraction of an inch. She was still pressed against Warnes and, with her paws, was still holding the woman's hand.

DOTTIE, the first Akita ever used as a guide dog in the United States, had an exceptionally demanding life with

Jeffrey Fowler. A cardiologist, legally blind since medical school, Fowler worked long days in Louisville, Kentucky. Sometimes he arrived home from the hospital at 3:30 in the morning, slept two hours, and got up to go back to his patients. No matter how difficult his schedule, Dottie, a galumphing teddy bear of a dog, guided him.

With the help of a closed-circuit magnifying television camera, Fowler read his patients' cardiograms and test results. With the help of Dottie, he read his patients' moods and recognized who needed extra soothing. Dottie, wandering in and out of exam rooms, visited worried patients in Fowler's office. While he went over lab data or dictated progress notes at the hospital, she searched out distressed people in the emergency, recovery, and waiting rooms.

Or in intensive care. A frail, elderly woman, lying in bed after a coronary bypass operation, could not speak to Fowler because she had a tube down her throat. So she scrawled a message on a piece of paper and gave it to his nurse: "Could Dottie come and visit?"

"Of course," Fowler said.

Fowler called Dottie, who had already met the woman in his office. The dog trotted into the room and went about her usual nursing: whimpering greetings, nuzzling the woman as best she could through the bed rail, and pressing herself against it, so the woman could reach through for "fur therapy."

The next day, when the woman's tube had been removed and she could speak, she asked again to see the dog. Dottie returned and tried to cheer her. When the patient stuck her hand through the bed rail to pet her, Dottie whined and licked her fingers.

On the third morning after the woman's surgery, Fowler was so busy dictating orders and writing a progress report in her chart that he paid little attention to Dottie. She, however, sensed that the patient still needed her and wandered in to visit. Dottie also seemed to know that the woman was feeling better. The Akita stood on her back legs and leaned—all hulking ninety-five pounds of her—onto the patient's bed. The woman circled her arms around Dottie, buried her face in her fur, and hugged her.

IN *Real Living with Multiple Sclerosis,* Penny Gillett Silvius describes Francine, her golden retriever service dog, who for years helped her get along in her wheelchair. As Silvius's illness made her too weak to use her legs and arms—or even to speak—she was confined to bed. Though Francine could do less for her than she had before, she did whatever she could and was always attentive.

As Silvius leaned toward her nightstand one evening, she toppled over and slowly began to slide out of bed. Her arms flopped in front of her head, but she could neither push herself back under the covers nor shout for help.

If no one pushed her back into bed, she was certain that she'd crash, headfirst, onto her concrete floor. Only a felt pad and a thin carpet would cushion the blow. At best, she was about to be covered with bruises.

"Lord, Lord, Lord," she mentally cried out. If only God would save her.

She made the only noise her lips and vocal cords still allowed her to utter: "Psst. Psst. Psst."

As she slid closer to the floor, she said it again: "Psst. Psst."

The sound was barely audible, and Silvius did not intend it as a call for Francine. Nevertheless, asleep in another room, the dog heard her. Francine raised her head and got to her feet. Silently, she came into Silvius's bedroom to see what was needed. For a moment Francine stood beside her. Then the dog moved closer as if she were trying to figure out how to help.

Although in service-dog training Francine had never been taught to help someone to bed, with her muzzle she gently nudged Silvius, then pushed with all her strength. Gradually, Francine raised Silvius enough that she could flop her arms over the dog's back. Then, with exquisite skill, Francine pushed the woman into bed again.

The Lord had heard her, Silvius believed. Through Francine's kindness, the Lord had saved her.

———

IN FRONT of the Dallas Independent School District's headquarters, a crowd of teenagers were shouting to protest teachers being fired. Darryl Crow and three other police officers were called in to calm the students. Slowly and cautiously the officers filed through a closed-off area for police and, on horseback, prepared to confront the demonstrators.

With tires screeching, a blue car suddenly turned the corner. The teenage driver sped down the street and fishtailed out of control—heading straight toward Crow and his horse, Tom Tom. Every muscle in Crow's body tensed. He was sure that Tom Tom would bolt and run; from behind, the car would mow them down.

Tom Tom, a shiny, copper-colored sorrel, had been trained to face a threat, so his rider could protect himself, just as Crow now needed him to do. But the man had only borrowed Tom Tom that morning because his own horse was sick; today was the first time Crow had ever been on Tom Tom's back. Surely, Crow could not rely on a horse who hardly knew him for protection—especially a horse who, as any frightened animal, wanted nothing more than to run away from danger and save himself.

Yet Tom Tom showed more concern for Crow's safety than his own and stood still as the car careened toward him. The horse did his duty for a stranger: Without flinching, he faced the car down.

The teenage driver slammed into Tom Tom so hard that the horse was thrown onto the car's hood. Crow, still on the horse's back, landed against the top of the windshield. When the car stopped, Crow, not badly hurt, rolled off, but Tom Tom tumbled to the pavement. His whole body quivering with pain, he struggled up and limped to a vacant lot across the street.

The car had slashed him in dozens of places. One of his rear legs had broken in half at the joint between his ankle and hoof. Crow ran to help him, but all he and the other officers could do for the horse was wrap a bandanna

around the break and apply pressure to hold the leg in place until they could get him to a veterinarian.

Tom Tom waited stoically for a horse trailer. He hobbled into it on his three good legs, then rode, badly suffering, for three long hours to Texas A&M's veterinary hospital. For even more hours, he waited while the police corporal who'd accompanied him made telephone calls to get funds approved for Tom Tom's surgery.

Finally, late into the night, ten veterinarians, assistants, and anesthesiologists sutured Tom Tom's cuts and fused bone from his hip onto his joint to hold it in place. By 2 A.M. the horse could stand, although he was in agonizing pain, which continued for months as the hospital's therapists tried to help him walk normally again. To compensate for his injured joint, Tom Tom leaned on his good leg and caused that hoof to become inflamed and weak. Soon it was almost as painful as his fracture.

Crow often came to visit Tom Tom at the hospital. Grateful for the horse's courage and protection, Crow hugged and patted him. But the visits were extremely distressing because Tom Tom was so obviously suffering. The joy had drained from the horse's face; his spirit seemed dark. Crow's spirit was dark as well when he drove home; he always returned to Dallas feeling sad.

Although some horses do not have the strength of will to overcome their injuries, Tom Tom kept bravely fighting to recover. Eventually, he became well enough to return to the police-horse barn, where, eager to please, he did whatever his trainer, Corporal Tom Hall, asked of him. No matter how sore and stiff Tom Tom was, or how miserably he limped each morning, he obeyed Hall's commands to walk, trot, and canter around the arena.

After months of work, he regained the stamina and confidence needed to patrol the streets again. Or so Hall thought. But within a year, even on a modified schedule, Tom Tom limped so badly that the police department retired him and sent him to work with children as a rehabilitation horse. Again, he tried hard to measure up to what was asked of him. Day after day, week after week, Tom Tom patiently circled a track with kids riding him.

No matter how bravely he stood up to his lameness, he continued to get worse. His limping was painful not just for him, but for anyone who watched him try so hard to keep going. Finally, veterinarians at Texas A&M removed some of the screws in his ankle to help him walk with less anguish. At first the surgery seemed to work, but then Tom Tom hobbled even more than before.

Both of his hind legs were aching. He revealed his pain with every step he took.

Six years after the teenage driver hit Tom Tom, a veterinarian finally put him down. For trying so hard to protect Officer Darryl Crow, Tom Tom had suffered way beyond the call of duty.

CHAPTER FOURTEEN

EXQUISITE
PERCEPTION

I N *CANINE GRAPEVINE,* Nancy Sciotti related this story of Lorenzo Abundiz, a southern California fireman, who took his rottweilers, Cinder and Reeno, to hike in the San Bernardino mountains one warm May day. Panting, the dogs padded along the trail beside him.

Cinder lagged behind. She whimpered, sat down, and refused to follow Abundiz. When he called her, she turned around and started back down the mountain. She stopped, then returned. Staring at him, she sat on the trail again.

Usually Cinder paraded in front of Abundiz and Reeno. She led the way instead of slowing them down. But now she clearly did not to want to take a hike. She seemed preoccupied, distracted.

Cinder had been a gift to Abundiz after he rescued two of his firemen colleagues from a half-ton burning wall that fell on them. With adrenaline pumping, he rushed through the smoke, lifted the wall with just one hand, and dragged the men out with the other. In gratitude, one of the men had presented him with Cinder.

Ever since she was a pup, she'd loved to go on hikes. Yet now she seemed to want only to go home. When she became more and more insistent about not climbing higher on the trail, Abundiz relented. The dog might be sick, he worried. He didn't want to force her to keep going if she didn't feel well.

Abundiz and Reeno turned around, followed Cinder to the car, and headed home. In the living room, Cinder planted herself on the floor near Abundiz and kept her brown eyes riveted on him. More certain than ever that something must be wrong with her, he started toward the telephone to call the veterinarian.

Suddenly his heart began pounding in his chest. The room went black. Scarcely able to breathe, Abundiz collapsed, unconscious, on the floor. When he came to, Reeno was licking his face. Abundiz was so weak that he could not move or call his wife, Roxanne.

Cinder recognized the crisis. As Abundiz lay, ashen, on the floor, she ran to the kitchen and nudged the portable telephone off the counter with her nose. She carried the phone across the room in her mouth, dropped it near Abundiz, and pushed it the rest of the way to his outstretched hand.

Punching 911 with his thumb took all his strength. He gasped to the dispatcher that he was having a heart attack.

Paramedics soon arrived with oxygen and drug injections that kept his heart going. An ambulance rushed him to the hospital in time for doctors to save his life. As Abundiz slowly recovered, he thought constantly about Cinder's concern for him. If she had not realized that he was about to be so sick—and insisted that he come down from the mountain—he'd have passed out somewhere on the trail, so close to death but so far from help.

AN ANIMAL watches the people it cares about with utmost attentiveness. The animal's great sensitivity enables it to pick up subtle changes in body language, smell, sound, and behavior—changes that predict the onset of an illness. When an animal perceives that people are getting sick, it often tries to alert them to the potential danger. The creature may jump on them, pace, bark, whine, misbehave, or stare at them with apprehension.

Another example of an animal who warned a person of illness was Jessie, a golden retriever in North Dakota. After Pamela Woodbeck brought her home to be a service dog, for weeks Jessie dutifully picked things up off the floor for Woodbeck, helped her open doors, and kept her wheelchair from tipping over. The dog also became extremely attached to her.

One day Woodbeck suddenly turned white and stared off into space. A short while later she got a migraine headache so severe that it was almost like a seizure. In misery, she went to bed for several days.

Jessie watched her with evident concern. Perhaps she associated Woodbeck's pain with other warning signals of the migraine: Chemical changes in Woodbeck's brain before the headache, for instance, might have triggered an unusual odor that Jessie smelled. Whatever the signals, the dog apparently realized that they meant Woodbeck would need extra care. And Jessie was ready to provide it.

Weeks later, when Woodbeck was sitting in her wheelchair, Jessie put her paws on her lap, looked into her face, and cocked her russet-brown eyebrow. She paced back and forth from Woodbeck to her bed so many times and with such urgency that Woodbeck realized Jessie wanted her to lie down. An hour later, Woodbeck felt the onset of a migraine. Jessie had known it was coming.

From then on, whenever a headache was about to start, the dog tried to get Woodbeck to bed.

IN *CAT FANCY,* Michelle Gomez related a story about her cat's diagnostic powers. Meep was an extraordinarily shy cat, so unassertive that Gomez had to coax her into being petted. But one morning she turned into an aggressive lion.

When Gomez got out of bed, turned on the television, and settled on the sofa to watch her favorite game show, Meep charged into the room. She leaped through the air onto Gomez' and dug her claws into her breast. Stunned by the viciousness—and by the pain—Gomez pushed the cat away.

To ease the aching, Gomez rubbed her bleeding breast. She felt a lump. Alarmed, she called her doctor.

After mammograms, a lumpectomy, and lab analysis of her breast tissue, she learned that she had an extremely aggressive type of cancer. If Meep had not pointed out the lump to her, her doctor told her, in a year she probably would have died.

MEEP IS not the only animal who has warned of cancer. A woman in London was surprised that her dog, Boo, kept sniffing at a mole on her leg with such unrelenting determination that she finally got the dog's message, went to her doctor, and learned that the mole was malignant.

George, a giant schnauzer in Tallahassee, Florida, did just as great a favor for Eddie Messer; however, George was being specifically taught to detect cancer.

During one of George's lessons, his trainer, Duane Pickel, held out a test tube of cancer cells for the dog to smell. Then Pickel set him free to sniff Messer, who was lying facedown on a table in a bathing suit—with bandages stuck all over his back. Under just one of them, Pickel had put cancer cells, and he hoped that George would find them. But George ignored them. Instead, he kept sniffing at another bandage over a freckle that Messer had seen a doctor about weeks before; the doctor had assured him that the freckle was not serious.

George kept sniffing and sniffing that bandage, pawing at it, and staring at Pickel to get his attention. When Pickel urged George to move on to the other bandages, the dog refused. His nose went straight back to the one over the freckle.

Lying there, Messer kept feeling George's wet nose, then his paw at that spot. George seemed to be doing so much more than simply trying to carry out his job, Messer thought. What struck him most was how eager the dog was to help, how desperately he seemed to want Messer and Pickel to take notice.

"It seems so important for him to show us the bandage," Messer told Pickel.

At George's urging, Messer went back to his doctor for a second look at the freckle. The diagnosis: third-degree malignant melanoma.

SEIKO, a standard black poodle, was brought into a desperate situation. As a service dog in Canada, he was enlisted to help Sue, who sometimes had twenty to thirty seizures a day, most likely a result of injuring her head in childhood.

During seizures, Sue had fallen down stairs, broken both feet, burned her legs, gotten hit by a car, and been mugged. After someone robbed her a second time, she was too apprehensive to go outside and stayed home for weeks. Her seizures became so frequent and severe that her children were frightened of being alone with her.

Seiko's arrival gave Sue and her family new hope. Perhaps he'd make all their lives more tolerable, they thought. He was carefully trained to recognize when Sue had a seizure that required immediate medical attention; then he knew to push a button till he heard a modem's high-pitched whine, acknowledging that an ambulance was coming. If Sue was away from the modem and had a seizure outdoors, Seiko also knew to stand guard over her and bark to prevent robberies— until help arrived or until Sue was conscious enough to command him, "Off."

In just a few months, Seiko saved Sue's life many times. Her family was immensely relieved, and Sue was ecstatic. She adored the dog.

Seiko apparently felt the same way about her. After eight months of his conscientious caretaking, he became so attached to her that he was able to predict—before she or anyone around her knew—that she was about to have a seizure. Though she herself could feel one coming for only about fifteen seconds before it struck, the dog was aware up to half an hour ahead of time.

With no training at all, Seiko began warning her of seizures by gently pinning her to the ground to keep her from moving, falling, or hurting herself when the seizure began. Sometimes, after it was over and she told him, "Off," he refused to move, knowing another seizure was on its way. Instead, he licked her hands and nuzzled her until the second seizure came and passed.

If he and Sue were walking outside as a seizure was about to start, Seiko would not move forward, no matter how severely she commanded him. He plopped on the ground and forced her to stop. If she insisted that they keep walking, he obeyed but continued to sit stubbornly again at shorter and shorter distances: every twenty feet, every ten, and finally every five. Sue became adept at gauging how soon her seizure would begin according to how many steps Seiko took between stops.

So sensitive and compassionate, he had figured out on his own the best way to take care of her. Says Sue, "Seiko has given me a life worth living."

LATE ONE NIGHT, Karen Brazelton was working in her office at Able, Inc., a Dickinson, North Dakota, group home for five disabled people. As she went about her business, the home's residents slept in their rooms with their doors shut. The house was quiet.

Yet Brazelton, who is hearing impaired, was unaware of the silence—and of the home's lilac Siamese-lynx cat, Shoo Shoo, who had jumped down from his sleeping spot on the living room sofa and was prowling the halls. The cat walked to the residents' bedrooms, sniffed and pawed at one of the doors, then hurried back to Brazelton's office. He sat in her doorway as if he were laying a siege and whipped his fluffy platinum tail to get her attention. Not realizing that he was especially agitated, she kept working.

Shoo Shoo had lived in Brazelton's own home until her children grew up and moved away. Because she and her husband worked all day, the cat became lonely and despondent. So Brazelton brought him to live at Able, where he quickly charmed the residents by stealing their pens with his teeth, sneaking drinks from their glasses, and whipping his tail in their faces.

Now at Brazelton's office door, he narrowed his blue eyes and glowered at her. She glanced at him but did not get up and go to him. Being ignored seemed to frustrate him more than ever. He ran along the hall to the residents' bedrooms, then raced back to her doorway. Again he whipped his tail through the air and thumped it on the floor. When Brazelton stayed at her desk, he turned his back to her and charged down the hall to the bedrooms again.

Brazelton finally realized that he wanted her to follow him. She also knew that all the residents in the house were asleep with their doors closed. Shoo Shoo, who had been sleeping in the living room, had no way of knowing what was happening with anyone in the house because he could not see them. But he was insistent about her following him to their rooms.

The cat had been just as insistent one morning when he ran around the house in a fury, meowed, threw himself at Brazleton, and refused to calm down. Thinking he'd gone crazy, she'd followed him and found a resident having seizures. From that day on, he patrolled the house. Once he'd even circled a resident's room for two nights and made such a pest of himself that Brazelton finally checked the woman's eyes and skin and found a yellowish cast; doctors in the emergency room diagnosed a dangerous liver dysfunction.

Brazelton got up from her chair and followed Shoo Shoo toward the bedrooms. She went to the door of the resident who most often had seizures; but when she opened it, she found the person sleeping peacefully. Shoo Shoo still wasn't satisfied, however. He led Brazelton to another door, scratched at it, and meowed. When Brazelton opened the door, she found that the resident on the bed was shaking and having a seizure.

Shoo Shoo tore into the room, put his paws on the edge of the woman's bed, and lay his head on her mattress. Brazelton stayed with her until the seizure passed, and Shoo Shoo also kept vigil at the bedside. Finally, when the woman was alert and feeling well again, the cat left her and went back to his usual sleeping spot on the living room sofa.

CHAPTER FIFTEEN

KINDNESS
to KIDS

BELLE, a black Labrador retriever in Lunenburg, Nova Scotia, was obedient and loving. Not *once* did Belle refuse to come when called. Like a loyal guard, she protected Kenny Knickles, age three, and followed him everywhere.

"I'm going out to play," Kenny told his mother, Nancy, one winter morning.

She looked up from the newspaper at the kitchen table. "Have fun."

Belle filed out the door behind Kenny. Besides watching after him, she kicked soccer balls to him, retrieved his hockey pucks, and hauled him around the yard on a sleigh by a rope clenched in her teeth. When Belle accompanied Kenny, Nancy never worried.

She finished the newspaper and talked for a moment on the telephone, then got up to check on Kenny. He and Belle, she discovered, had left the yard. While she'd been on the phone, they'd probably gotten cold and come back inside. Nancy searched the house, but they were both missing.

Nancy walked through the snow to the nearby woods where they usually played. She found no trace of them. When she shouted their names, Kenny did not answer. What was even more cause for alarm was that Belle did not come. Worried, Nancy hurried back home and phoned her neighbors, but no one had seen Kenny and Belle.

Panicked, Nancy telephoned her husband, Kenneth, at his office. "They *have* to be lost in the woods," she insisted.

"Did you look around the channel?" The Lunenburg Harbour Channel, which then would have been at half-tide and about ten feet deep, bordered the Knickles' property.

"They never go anywhere near the water. They can't be there," Nancy reassured Kenneth—and herself.

As Kenneth hurried home, his mind circled around all the possibilities of where his son might be and why Belle hadn't come to Nancy's call. Crossing the bridge over the channel, he glanced down into the partly frozen water and was stunned to see Belle hanging by her claws to an icy ledge along the bank. Only her head and paws were visible above the slush.

Belle could easily have let go of the bank and swum to safety. Instead, Kenneth was certain, with her black body against the white snow, that she was marking the spot where his son could be found. Hanging there, she wanted someone to see her and come to rescue Kenny. Using her body as a signal, she was calling for help.

Kenneth parked the car and ran to help her, drenched and shivering, onto the bank. When he put his head into the water to look under a crust of ice for Kenny, he saw one of his son's Mickey Mouse mittens at the bottom of the channel.

Kenneth's heart beat with such force that his temples pounded. As Belle whined, he threw his hat into the water to see which direction it would float—and which direction the water might have pulled Kenny under the ice. Following the hat with his eyes, Kenneth spotted a small piece of Kenny's blue snowsuit on the channel's surface *just eight feet from where Belle had been hanging.* The boy had turned upside down in the water. Air that was trapped under his suit barely kept him afloat.

Just as Kenneth saw his son, Belle jumped back into the water and swam to save him. Nancy ran to the channel while Kenneth leaped across it from chunk to chunk of ice. Lying on a thick frozen slab to anchor himself, he pulled Belle, then Kenny out of the water. Belle watched as Kenneth frantically pushed on Kenny's chest; water gushed out of the boy's mouth.

Kenneth picked the boy up and jumped back across floating ice cakes to shore. Certain that his son was dead, he was numb with shock. Nancy buried her face in her hands and sobbed. Belle barked as if she were calling for help.

When firemen arrived, the dog was so excited to see them that she whimpered, leaped on them, and tried to get into the ambulance with Kenny's lifeless body. As the ambulance sped away, she ran after it until Nancy and Kenneth forced her to come back home, where she paced from room to room and seemed lost and inconsolable.

Nancy and Kenneth put her in the basement and drove, grief-stricken, to the hospital. They believed that the doctors would never be able to bring Kenny back to life.

"He was in the water half an hour," a doctor told them. "If we revive him, he'll be brain dead."

Doctors tried to revive him anyway. Although they got Kenny's heart beating, they were not optimistic. Kenny, they warned, had "a five percent chance of making it."

For days as Kenny fought for his life, Kenneth and Nancy traveled back and forth to the hospital. Belle moped at home. Occasionally, she walked to the channel and looked across the water, perhaps to see if Kenny was there. She ran around the yard as if she were searching for him, then sat on the front stoop and watched the road for him.

After three weeks, he came home—without brain damage. A miracle.

Another miracle had been Belle's intelligence and sacrifice. For weeks the Knickles asked themselves, "What if? . . ." What if Belle had left Kenny in the channel and had come to Nancy's call? And what if the tide had dragged Kenny away under the ice while Belle was gone? Then, even the dog might not have known where Kenny was. If she'd not hung, wet and shivering, onto the bank to mark the spot, Kenneth never would have found his son in time.

Although Belle loved the water as much as most retrievers do, she never again swam in the channel where Kenny had almost drowned. Occasionally, she stood on the bank and barked at the water. Remembering? Warning Kenny to stay away? Still protecting him from danger? No one knew for sure.

BRUNO, a German shepherd, padded along behind eleven-year-old Donnie Skiffington as he rode his bicycle around his family's cabin in Princeton, Newfoundland. Then he took a different route, pedaled down a hill, and accidentally hit a rock, which thrust the bike into his face and knocked him out. He flew through the air into a ditch at the bottom of the hill, where he lay tangled in his bicycle, blood pouring from gashes around his eye and on his forehead.

Bruno ran to him, hovered over him, and licked the blood off his face as he slowly regained consciousness. Still, Donnie was too disoriented and in too much pain to call his parents for help. Bruno did it for him. He ran to Donnie's mother, Cindy, grabbed her hand, and tried to pull her down the hill to Donnie. Thinking the shepherd was just being playful—though annoying—she ignored him and went back to her chores.

Bruno refused to give up. He hurried back to Donnie, still traumatized and bleeding on the ground. As the boy started to cry, Bruno apparently made a decision: If he could not bring help *to* Donnie, he would bring

Donnie to *help*. Bruno grabbed the boy's shirt collar in his teeth and dragged him out of the ditch and up the hill. Just then Donnie's father, Eric, looked up from the wood he was chopping and saw the dog's desperate tugging.

Eric and Cindy took Donnie to the hospital, where twenty stitches were needed to close his wounds. When Donnie got home, the German shepherd lay at his feet and watched after him like a solicitous nurse.

———

JENNY, a muscled, one-hundred-pound rottweiler, liked to hang around Veronica Retana, who was the baby-sitter on a Pound Ridge, New York, estate. The dog followed her and the children from room to room. No matter how rough the children got with Jenny, she let them crawl all over her.

One afternoon, a man with a red pony tail and a thin red mustache knocked on the door. "I'm here to pick up the baby."

Its father, the man explained, had just had an accident and was being rushed to the hospital. The mother, on her way to join him, wanted her baby there with her.

Retana studied the stranger's fleshy, pock-marked face and saw her own face reflected in his sunglasses. Suspicious that he was lying to her, she told him to wait at the door while she called the baby's mother.

Retana partly closed the door and went back inside the house to the telephone. Jenny lay on the floor guarding the baby. The man shoved the door open, walked into the living room, and grabbed the infant. As the man ran away, Jenny chased him down the driveway to a white van, where a woman waited with the motor running.

To keep the man from getting into the van with the baby, Jenny ran circles around him, barked, snapped, and jumped on him. When he resisted, she clamped her teeth into his arm. He dropped the baby, screaming, on the lawn. As the man jumped in the van and sped away, Retana tore out of the house. The rottweiler was gently sniffing the baby. Though she was crying, she was unhurt.

―――

ANIMALS CAN be extremely sensitive to children. Besides trying to rescue them in emergencies, creatures often try to help them when they're lost. The animals stay with them and keep them warm until someone finds them, or else the animals lead other people back to them.

• Lady, a collie–German shepherd mutt, followed three-year-old Tommy Abel, who was lost in the woods in suburban St. Louis. When Tommy became mired in a swamp, he tried desperately to free himself. But by sunset, as the temperature dropped, he'd sunk down to his knees in clay and was so exhausted that he couldn't even shout for help.

Frantic to help him, Lady ran through the woods and found two telephone linemen. She whined and bolted back toward Tommy, then back to the men again and again until they understood that she wanted them to come with her. They picked up their equipment, followed, and found Tommy, still sinking. After pulling him free, they brought him home with Lady.

• Ringo, part St. Bernard and perhaps part chow, became agitated when Randy Saley, age two-and-a-half, sat down, lost, in the middle of a busy road, just beyond a blind curve a mile from his house. Ringo stationed himself at the curve and blocked cars before they could hit Randy. If the cars didn't stop quickly enough, *Ringo threw himself at their fenders.*

Ringo repeatedly hastened back to Randy and tried to nudge him to the curb. Each time, Randy thought Ringo was playing—and ran back to the middle of the road. But, Ringo was *not* playing. In fifteen minutes, he had lined up forty cars behind the curve. He was so exhausted trying to protect Randy that he shuffled, panting, along the asphalt.

Harley Jones, one of the drivers, walked to the head of the cars and found Randy. After calming Ringo down, Jones picked up the little boy and carried him to the curb. Yet with each step, Ringo kept his mouth around Jones's calf and was ready to bite him if Jones hurt Randy. Only when the child was safe and about to be taken home, did Ringo let the forty cars pass.

• When Joe Stadler was irrigating his hay fields in Oakdale, California, his border collie mix, named Mutt, trotted along behind him and sniffed the canal bank. Mutt suddenly stopped, raised his head, and stared down the slope toward the water. He clambered down-hill to a white bump hidden in the grass.

Mutt's whimpering and wagging his tail seemed to indicate that something was wrong. He was going to investigate. Stadler followed him to the bump; the white object was a towel with Garfield cats printed on the terry cloth, and wrapped in the towel was an abandoned baby. Says Stadler, "Mutt knew the little human needed help."

———

BEN, a golden retriever, lay, as always, under the desk of Virginia attorney Wayne Sawyers. When two broth-ers, ages eight and nine, entered the office, the dog panted eagerly and looked up at Sawyers for permission to greet them. They sat down, stiff as nails, on the sofa.

Sawyers, who had been appointed the boys' tempo-rary guardian during their parents' divorce, was sup-posed to talk with them and establish which parent should have custody, then make the case for that parent in court. The brothers had never met Sawyers before. Distrustful and nervous, they stared at the rug and at the stitching on their loafers. One brother cleared his throat.

"Are you scared of dogs?" Sawyers asked.

"No."

"Okay, then. Benny! Go get 'em!"

Benny came out from behind the desk. As he usu-ally did when meeting children, he jumped up and down, wagged his tail, and made a little roar to ask for petting. Then he nuzzled the boys with his licoricegumdrop nose. As he licked their cheeks, their faces softened into smiles.

"He's my service dog," Sawyers said. "He knows how to turn on lights. He carries my papers in his teeth to court bailiffs."

Listening, the boys looked directly at Sawyers for the first time.

"He's brought me an unweaned kitten and a baby rabbit with a broken leg," Sawyers said. "He wanted me to help them."

"Did you?"

"Sure."

The boys' trust of Sawyers rose another notch.

"Do you have pets?" he asked.

As the boys described their cat and gerbil, they ran their fingers through Ben's golden fur. Soon they were rolling on the floor with him and laughing at his playful yips.

Little by little, Sawyers worked the conversation around to more serious questions: What do you do when you come home from school? Does your mother help you with your lessons? Has your father quit drinking?

As the boys answered, Ben stood by, a panting security blanket.

After several visits with the brothers, Sawyers went to court with Ben to suggest joint custody.

"All rise," the bailiff ordered.

Ben rose with everyone else in the room, as the dog always did when a judge walked to the bench.

CHAPTER SIXTEEN

FAVORS
to STRANGERS

I ASKED MARC BEKOFF, a University of Colorado animal behaviorist, "Why are animals kind to us?"

His explanation focused on dogs. "They're part of the family," he said. "I see my dog as my kin. He sees me as kin, too."

In other words, just as people naturally help their relatives and close friends, creatures also come to the aid of those they feel close to. The animals are concerned about the well-being of people in their human families.

Yet this theory does not account for all of the times that animals have been kind to strangers. Creatures of many species have shown compassion to people they've never even seen before.

One dog found a woman lying unconscious on an equestrian trail; he sat beside her and barked nonstop until he attracted the attention of someone who would help. Other dogs ran to get assistance for strangers in other kinds of danger—two young boys who were clinging to an overturned canoe in choppy, freezing water; a teenager who was entangled in mountain-climbing ropes, hanging from a cliff; and a man who was bleeding and trapped under a 2,680-pound scraper tire in a deserted warehouse.

———

TARA, a German shepherd in Duncan, British Columbia, was roaming through the woods one day when a motorcycle sped down a nearby train track. At a crossing, the rider hit a railroad tie that had been placed parallel to the track and lost control of his bike. His body flew through the air and landed with a thud. Nearly comatose, he moaned from pain. The accident had crushed his knees and elbows.

Tara pricked her ears, approached the tracks, and listened intently. The moans convinced her that someone was in trouble. Dashing home to Helmut Langer, who was working in a warehouse behind the house, she barked so persistently that he could not ignore her.

Langer finally got up from his desk and looked out the window. Tara stared at him, then headed toward the railroad tracks. After going only a short distance, she stopped and looked back at him again. The German shepherd obviously wanted him to follow. She seemed determined to convey her message.

Outside, Langer hurried after Tara and heard muffled cries for help. In the middle of the tracks lay the young man, immobilized after his motorcycle accident. Even though he was a stranger to Tara, she stood by him until the paramedics took him to a hospital.

Twenty minutes later, a train thundered down the tracks.

———

VEDA RHYNE returned home from church in Gastonia, North Carolina, and let Spud, her energetic little cocker spaniel–hound, outside to run free in the neighborhood. Spud's ears, which sometimes stood erect and sometimes flopped, bounced with his loping rhythm as he took off down the street. Sniffing, he skimmed his nose along the asphalt.

After going a quarter of a mile, Spud came upon a man lying in the grass near a lawn mower. Mark Pruitt had suffered a heart attack while mowing his yard. No one had heard his feeble yells for help.

Spud crossed a ditch and scurried over to a house on the other side, then circled around to the front porch where Ruth Moore was rocking in her chair. Spud barked, gave a pleading whine, and tore around the house again.

"Is somebody back there in my garden?" Moore asked him.

Her question was not really serious. No one was in her garden, she was certain. She continued rocking as Spud disappeared, returned, sat beside her, and yapped again. When he ran behind her house a second time, she became worried. He was so desperate to communicate something. Maybe someone *was* there.

Moore walked through her house to the back door and looked outside to the garden. Although no one was in the garden, she could see Pruitt lying in the grass past the ditch. Spud, standing beside him, was still barking.

"Is anything wrong?" Moore shouted to Pruitt.

"Help me!"

Moore called an ambulance.

The next December Pruitt brought Spud a Christmas stocking filled with rawhide chewies. Pruitt was still amazed that Spud had run to a stranger to get help for a stranger. God, Pruitt decided, had enlisted the little mongrel to spare his life for a reason. Pruitt was still trying to figure out what that reason was.

———

ONE DAY a young woman was outside washing windows for her employer in Spencer, Indiana. A giant of a man—at least six-foot-six and weighing over three hundred pounds—appeared out of nowhere. Even on that chilly afternoon, he wore no shirt under his bib overalls, the legs of which were stuffed in muddy combat boots. He was grubby and disheveled.

The mere sight of him intimidated the woman. Her prickly sense of danger proved to be right, but she had no time to escape. He pulled out a knife and held it to her throat.

"Get in the truck," he ordered and pushed her behind the wheel of her employer's pickup. "Start the engine."

In terror, she turned the key.

After she had driven to the edge of town, the man pointed to a deserted logging road. "Turn there."

She turned onto the road. Not far ahead a house came into sight. The logging road was a driveway. She prayed that someone would be home.

When the man commanded her to back down the hill, she was trembling so badly that she could barely shift into reverse. About a hundred feet from the house, she rolled into a ditch. No matter how much she tried to accelerate, the truck stayed mired in the mud.

The man's face flushed with rage. "Get out," he snapped.

To make sure she obeyed, he flashed his knife and shoved her out the door. As they walked up the hill toward overgrown woods, the woman panicked. In such a dark, remote place, no one would ever rescue her. After the man had finished with her, no one would even *find* her. She was so frightened that her lungs refused to fill with air, but she kept walking.

At that moment, Bruno, a muscular German shepherd mix with legs not much longer than a basset hound's, was wandering through the woods. Despite having such short legs, the dog was agile enough to climb his fence, escape from his yard, and patrol the more extended acres of Louis Brown's property. As Bruno explored the sassafras and sycamore, he noticed a man shoving a woman on the road. Perhaps she reminded the dog of Brown's daughters, whom Bruno had always protected.

Bruno, growling, charged the man and lunged for his throat. Screaming as the dog's teeth sank into his neck, the man released the woman and fled. But Bruno hadn't finished with him. He pursued the man down the road as the woman ran, sobbing, toward the house she'd just passed. The owner immediately called the sheriff.

An intensive search for the woman's abductor led nowhere. Someone matching his description was picked up in a lumber yard, then released. Whoever had terrorized the woman was never arrested.

A few years later Bruno wandered into the forest and roamed perhaps a little farther than he should. Someone shot him. Brown found his mutt tossed in a ditch with a bullet in his stomach. Bruno, who had tried so hard to *help* a stranger, had been *killed* by a stranger. To Brown, the injustice was devastating.

———

IN *ANIMAL HEROES*, Byron G. Wells described a young girl in Brooklyn's Prospect Park who mounted a horse for the first time in her life and cautiously rode along a winding bridle path. As she passed under a stone bridge, hooligans threw rocks down on her horse and spooked him. He broke into a wild gallop. The girl, shrieking, lost hold of his reins, and her feet slipped from the stirrups. She grabbed the horse's neck and clung to him.

Another rider raced after her and brought his horse alongside in order to slow her horse down. As the two horses galloped side by side, the man lifted the girl off her saddle to allow her frightened horse to run ahead without her. But instead of taking off, her horse paced itself with the man's horse. They finally stopped together.

After setting the girl on the ground, the man realized that his horse had grasped the other horse's reins in his teeth to slow him down.

———

ONE COOL morning in Dobbins, California, David Giles was running the clothes dryer in his garage. When he stepped outside for a moment, away from the motor's hum, he heard an odd sound, like a bird call, yet unlike the sound of any bird he'd ever come across before.

Usually, he could identify all the birds in the Sierra Nevada mountains that surrounded his house. This call was a mystery. He shrugged, puzzled, and with his nearly deaf German shepherd, Ernie, started back toward his garage.

Before stepping inside, he glanced at the edge of the yard, where it dropped into a steep canyon. Staring intently down into it from the lawn was his cat,

Bustopher Jones, a hefty black ruffian with a white "shirt front" and "spats."

Everything about the cat's expression and body language was saying, "There's something wrong down there," Giles thought uneasily. Bustopher was rigid and motionless. A frown wrinkled his forehead, his tail stuck straight out in a horizontal line, and he was pointing his right paw toward the trees below the yard. Pointing was a skill he'd recently acquired.

At the beginning of Giles's marriage to his wife, Marjorie, Bustopher had been an unseemly thug who shredded books, clawed his way up curtains, and used Giles's sofa for a scratching post and his Chinese carpet for a toilet. But moving into Marjorie's house had changed his behavior for the better. She'd sunk him into sheep dip to kill his fleas, and she let him roam outside to claw trees and dirt instead of furniture. Day by day, he'd become polite and considerate.

He had also picked up the odd habit of pointing like a bird dog. Whenever a deer wandered into the yard, the cat leaned back and aimed his right foot at the creature. Bustopher also pointed at birds, gophers, and moles.

Thinking perhaps that the cat had encountered some other animal, Giles crossed the lawn. When he was a few feet from the clothes-dryer noise, he heard the strange "bird" call again.

The closer Giles got to his cat, the more distinct the call sounded.

"Help me! Help me!" a woman cried faintly in the canyon. Her voice sounded at least a quarter of a mile away.

Giles left Bustopher, who still looked upset, and climbed with Ernie down into the canyon to investigate. As they traveled along a steep, circuitous route, Bustopher peered down at them.

"Help me!" the woman begged.

"I'm coming," Giles shouted.

"Thank God!" The woman started to cry.

As Giles got closer, he found Talma Crenshaw, age eighty-four, lying in a deep hole. She had gone down to turn off a faucet in her irrigation system and had fallen and broken her hip. For over an hour, she'd been lying on the cold ground in terrible pain and going in and out of consciousness.

Giles wrapped his jacket around her and ran to call an ambulance. He returned with paramedics.

"How did you ever hear me?" Crenshaw asked.

"I didn't. My cat did."

Looking down from the yard, Bustopher continued to oversee the rescue. He still appeared to be distressed about the stranger.

CHAPTER SEVENTEEN

THE ABILITY
to PREDICT

ALTHOUGH THUNDERSTORMS, one after another, had been passing through Rancho Arnaz, California, for days, the rain had finally ended, and the sun was out. Sandy LaChaine and his girlfriend, Leslie Harrison, set out to visit friends in the evening with no thought of floods or other hazards.

Sandy, with Leslie beside him, drove his Toyota truck onto a roadway that crossed San Antonio Creek. Normally, a tiny stream of water flowed over the road, and crossing it had never been a problem. Sandy carefully entered what he thought was shallow water, but in the darkness he could not see that storms had swollen the creek into a river. It engulfed the truck and flushed it, like a toy boat, off the roadway onto a sandbar.

The truck teetered precariously. At any moment, swift currents could have swept Sandy and Leslie into water over their heads. Shivering, they sat in the cab and tried to decide what to do. When water rose to the windshield, they knew that they had to do *something* immediately.

They crawled out the windows to the Toyota's bed, where they huddled together and screamed until their throats were raw. The water's roar was so loud that no one heard.

Except for Otto, a thirteen-pound dachshund puppy, who barked and yapped and tore around his house as if bombs were falling on it. His family, Linda and Larry Nass, ignored what they considered to be just another display of Otto's youthful hysteria. They assumed that he was only trying to scare away cars on the road and protect the house, as usual.

Otto, however, refused to tolerate their not responding. On stubby little legs, he trundled from room to room and worked himself into a yowling frenzy. No matter what Linda or Larry said to him, he would not give up his self-appointed mission as an emergency alarm. He filled his tiny lungs with air and barked with the importance of an elephant.

Larry finally gave in, got a flashlight, and went outside to see what had turned his gentle pet into a hyperactive maniac. Otto waddled ahead of him toward the creek bank and barked again.

Nass shined his flashlight into the creek and found Sandy and Leslie trapped in the truck bed. Nass scooped up Otto to stop his barking and prevent his accidentally falling in the water, then dashed into the house and phoned for help.

Within minutes, fire trucks, ambulances, and highway patrol cars arrived with flashing lights and wailing sirens.

The emergency crew extended a ladder to the Toyota, and Sandy and Leslie crawled above the water to the muddy bank. Several of the workers were eager to meet Otto, who was serene now that his rescue was finished. Sandy, thankful to be on dry land, hugged the pup.

The next day Sandy's mother, Maree LaChaine, went to examine the truck, which was still immersed in water. "My God!" she exclaimed. "They'd have drowned if they'd tried to cross the creek on their own."

Fortunately, they never had to. An attentive dachshund puppy had made sure of that.

CATS AND DOGS frequently help people during natural disasters. With an uncanny ability to predict the future, some creatures even give warnings *before* the danger strikes.

• Toto, an Italian tabby cat, meowed and clawed and ran back and forth through his house. After he finally got his family outdoors, Mount Vesuvius erupted. Toto's family watched in safety as molten lava crushed their village and killed thirty of their neighbors.

• Calliope, a cat described in *Cat Fancy* magazine, tore around her house and meowed to wake the woman in her family. When the woman did not get out of bed, Calliope jumped on her, licked her eyelids, and squawked in her face. Three minutes later, an earthquake shook the house.

• Buddy Ben, a German shepherd mix, woke as a tornado whirled outside the Lawton, Oklahoma, motor home of his family, Dave and Linda Hickam. Buddy Ben put his front paws on their bed, whined, and ran his huge tongue over their cheeks until they awoke. Then he leaped on Dave and pushed him out of bed—only seconds before the tornado threw another mobile home through the roof of his house exactly where he'd been lying.

HURRICANE FRAN had scarcely blown into Raleigh, North Carolina, but she was already shaking trees as if they were match sticks. After hearing disturbing forecasts on the television news, Eddie and Patti Clinton secured the umbrellas and patio furniture near their swimming pool, drew water with their pump in case trees fell and cut their power lines, and checked on their cat and their beagle, Mini, who slept together on the enclosed front porch. With an unsettling feeling, Eddie and Patti went to bed.

As wind churned in the trees, Eddie drifted off to sleep, but Patti, too worried to close her eyes, stayed awake reading. Outside on the porch, Mini whimpered.

Whimpered? Patti put down her book and strained to listen over the wind to her dog's mournful, muted cries. Once in a while, Mini barked or howled during the night, but whimper? Never. Surely, she was trying to get Patti's and Eddie's attention.

Mini had been abandoned in the woods near their house and had survived, alone, for three days before Patti even discovered her; she had been so tiny that she fit into Patti's hand. The pup had parasites, an injured leg, and an open, running sore on her side. For weeks Patti fed her with an eyedropper and kept her warm on a heating pad while she recovered.

As an adult, the beagle did her best to repay the kindness that had been lavished on her. When the Clinton's cat gave birth to a kitten with a broken back, Mini snuggled up to keep him warm and watched after him. At that very moment, while Hurricane Fran was blasting the trees outside, the two animals were surely cuddling, as they did each night, on the Clinton's porch.

But whimpering? Mini's sounds of distress changed Patti's unease to major concern. She got out of bed and walked across the room to the atrium door. As she looked out into the darkness to see what might have prompted Mini's whimpering, a tree blew down onto the roof.

Patti screamed. Instinctively, she threw herself at the door to get out of the way just as Eddie rolled off the bed onto the carpet—and the tree dropped straight through the ceiling. Its trunk landed exactly where they had been lying in bed.

They had no time to feel grateful for not being crushed. Wood chips and branches were flying through the air. Eddie sprang to his feet. He and Patti ran out of the bedroom. But no room was truly safe because a second tree crashed through the kitchen ceiling and another fell into the living room.

Outside, trees snapped in half and swirled, destroying everything near them. Frozen in shock, Eddie and Patti clung to each other. But they couldn't just stand there—they had to protect themselves and the animals. Mini had just saved their lives, and they wanted her inside.

Patti opened the front door to let Mini in, but she had disappeared. Even Patti's shouting from the porch brought no response. In the blackness—with power lines strewn all around the yard—looking for the dog outside was too risky. But the thought of Mini, alone and struggling to survive in the hurricane, was devastating. Patti imagined all the horrible things that could happen to her dog.

Nearly sick with worry, Patti and Eddie sat down on their hall floor with the cellular phone. After dialing dozens of times, Patti finally got through to 911.

"Are you okay?" the dispatcher asked.

"So far," Patti responded.

"So far is right. The brunt of the storm isn't even *here* yet."

Wonderful, Patti thought. Just what she wanted to hear when their house had already been half-destroyed and Mini was outside, defenseless. How could the wind, which sounded like a train rumbling toward them, possibly get worse? How could Mini survive?

For the next four hours, rain poured through the roof and drenched the carpet while trees struck the ground outside.

"Ten down," Eddie said.

"Stop counting the trees!" Patti insisted. "I can't take it anymore."

Especially since a tree might hit Mini. Images of her dog being crushed by a falling pine tree filled Patti's mind. In such a disaster, her beagle surely could not survive, Patti warned herself. She had to be prepared to lose her.

"Please don't die!" Patti mentally encouraged Mini, as she waited for the unrelenting wind to die down.

By 6 A.M., the eye of Hurricane Fran had completely passed through Raleigh. Since branches blocked all of the doors, the Clintons had to climb out a window to the backyard to search for their animals. They located their cat, but Mini was nowhere to be found. No matter how often or how loudly Patti called her, she did not come.

Despairing of ever seeing her dog again, Patti resigned herself to Mini's death. Just then a black nose appeared from the door of the dressing room next to the swimming pool. Mini, bedraggled and bloody, hobbled toward them.

A tree had fallen and gashed the beagle's head, but she was alive. In a few weeks her cut healed.

Patti often thinks about how much she owes Mini for her whimpered warning. "Ever since that night we've treated her like royalty," Patti says.

STELLA, a fluffy Samoyed with rust-tipped ears, was sleeping, as she always did, on the floor beside the bed of Myrna Huffman. When an earthquake, 6.8 on the Richter scale, struck Simi Valley, California, the house rocked on its foundation, and objects in every room clattered to the floor.

Surrounded by darkness, she opened her eyes. "My God!" she told herself. "This is the end of the world! Everyone is going to die!"

As the house swayed around her, Huffman, too petrified to move, trembled under her blanket. But Stella suddenly jumped to her feet. Instead of running to safety out the patio door, which was always left open for her, the dog leaped up beside Huffman to protect her. Never in the four years since she had rescued Stella from the pound, had the dog climbed onto the bed.

Even more unusual, Stella spread her body, like a shield, over Huffman's stomach. At that moment, a television set that had been sitting on a three-shelf unit above the bed fell to the floor. Seconds later, the 250-pound oak unit itself was loosened from its bolts. Instead of striking Huffman's stomach, the unit landed on Stella.

Huffman did not have a single scratch or bruise, but the shelf unit almost completely severed Stella's paw from her leg. In fact, all that prevented her paw from falling off was fur and skin. In agony, she quivered and whined, but she had accomplished her mission of saving Huffman.

Careful not to cause Stella any more pain, Huffman climbed out of bed, pushed the oak unit off the dog, and carried her outside. To ease Stella's shock, Huffman covered her with blankets. Because Stella was too weak to lift her head and lap water from a bowl, Huffman helped her drink from a turkey baster. Stella's pain made Huffman feel sick inside.

She had no idea how to help her dog in such a crisis. The phones were dead because of the earthquake. Daylight would not come for many hours. Even in the morning, the temblor would have damaged so many buildings in the area that no vets' offices would be open for injured animals.

Huffman sat beside Stella, patted her, and tried to comfort her. The dog's eyes were glazed, and she shivered with pain. As Huffman waited for morning, the hours seemed to crawl by on broken glass.

Not until noon—and until Stella had suffered for twelve hours—was Huffman able to get a dial tone on her telephone. She called a local radio station to ask where Stella could receive treatment. Huffman learned that a veterinarian, whose phone was not working, was attending to animals hurt in the earthquake. She quickly dialed her son-in-law, who arrived with his truck and laid Stella, limp and sick, in the back.

The vet took one look at the dog and immediately gave her several injections for her pain. Since the earthquake had cut off his electricity, he could not x-ray or repair her paw. For two more days Stella lay injured in a cage before he could ascertain how badly she'd been hurt. The wall unit had shattered her tendons and torn her ligaments, nerve endings, and blood vessels.

The vet fixed his serious eyes on Huffman. "You should put her down."

Huffman felt as if she'd been punched in the stomach.

"Repairing her paw would cost far too much," he continued.

"I don't *care* how much it costs," she insisted. "Do whatever you have to. Just help her."

"The surgery might not work. You could be wasting your money."

"I'd give up my home to pay for her surgery. Without her, I'd have been crushed to death."

The vet relented. For hours he operated on Stella's paw. He inserted screws in her bones to hold them together, and pinned, stitched, and worried.

Three months later, Stella was able to walk around Huffman's house again, but not without limping. Her disability would be permanent, a daily sacrifice she would make for showing compassion.

Had Stella sensed that the oak wall unit was going to fall on Huffman? Was that the reason the dog had leaped onto the woman and turned herself into a shield? Huffman is not sure whether dogs can foresee the future, but she suspects that Stella did.

CHAPTER EIGHTEEN

SENSITIVITY
to DISABILITY

WHEN JIM BIRD came home from the hospital after a heart-valve-replacement operation, he carried a pillow over his chest, as the doctors had insisted, to protect his newly stitched incision. Jim opened his front door and stepped into his house in Pt. Arena, California. His Samoyed–German shepherd, Kai, slinked up to him, sniffed the air around his leg to acknowledge him, and sat down, to watch him with lugubrious brown eyes.

"What's *wrong* with him?" Jim asked his wife, Pat.

Normally, as soon as Jim came through the door, the dog leaped on him, yipped enthusiastic greetings, and danced with joy around his legs. How long Jim had been absent was irrelevant. Kai welcomed him from a ten-minute trip to his garden just as ecstatically as from a three-week vacation.

"Kai must be trying not to hurt you," Pat reasoned. "He must know you're vulnerable."

Undoubtedly, Pat was right.

Kai had once been vulnerable himself. After Pat answered a newspaper ad for a "fluffy puppy" and had brought Kai home, she and Jim discovered that he had been fiercely beaten. Some cruel person had smashed the puppy's skull and had broken his jaw. A veterinarian had surely saved his life.

Because of Kai's difficult origins, he became a grateful and sensitive pet. Besides welcoming Jim home with yowls of pleasure, he greeted him every morning with a ritual as predictable as the sunrise. The instant Jim opened his eyes, Kai rose from his sleeping spot on the floor next to Jim's bed. Standing on his back legs, Kai rested his paws and chest against Jim's chest. For a few minutes, Jim and Kai hugged and reassured each other. Then Jim let the dog out for his morning stroll in the woods.

The morning after Jim was released from the hospital—for the first time since Kai had come to live with him—the dog did not jump up and put his paws on Jim's chest for a hug. Instead, he stood beside the bed and gently rested his muzzle on the pillow next to Jim's face—so close that Kai's whiskers tickled Jim's cheek.

Week after week, as Jim recovered from his surgery, Kai gave him this modified morning greeting so as to keep from hurting him. He restrained his exuberance and never jumped on Jim or pressed too closely against him. And Kai rarely left Jim's side. Pat had to call and cajole the dog to get him to come to the kitchen to eat. Kai, who normally had a ravenous appetite, was reluctant to leave Jim alone even briefly.

Kai also seemed to be aware of the pillow over Jim's chest. When Jim's surgical incision had finally healed enough to need the pillow only when he was driving, Kai sensed Jim's new vigor and knew that the danger had passed. One morning Kai woke, sat up on his back legs, and again reached his paws across Jim's chest to press his own chest against Jim's. At last, they could resume their morning hugs.

———

CREATURES CAN be astonishingly sensitive to physical disabilities. Many people have told me, "Animals just seem to *know* . . ." when our bodies are weak, vulnerable, or incapacitated. Nearly as many people have also insisted that one of the reasons animals were placed on the earth is to protect and encourage disabled people.

I agree.

Once I injured four disks in my spine and was confined to bed for many months. My tabby cat Linguine curled up into a striped ball at my feet and kept me company. She did not try to lie on my chest as she had for years; I suspected that she knew her weight might hurt me. Instead, she purred in her new spot and let me know that she was there, subtly present without intruding.

One bleak afternoon, I was so worn down by pain that even my soul felt gray and roughened at the edges. When I closed my eyes, all I could see was my life extending before me like a pot-holed road, leading only to more months of misery. Giving in to self-pity, I started to cry—not just a moderate sniveling, but a humdinger of an outburst. Tears soaked my cheeks, ears, and hair—then fell onto my turtleneck and made it soggy.

Linguine raised an eyelid and gazed at the air next to my head, as if her looking directly at me might seem like impolitely gawking at a hysteric. She got up and arched her back. Perhaps she thought that rushing to my assistance might make me feel she had no faith that I could help myself. She stepped softly across my blanket, curled up in the crook of my arm, and very gently pressed her little furry body against my ribs.

This incident reinforced my belief that animals are great gifts to us. They almost seem to be hanging around, specifically waiting for opportunities to help us—especially when we're physically disabled.

WHEN MARIE MURPHY'S iron lung suddenly stopped functioning in the middle of the night, she woke with a start. Polio had paralyzed her from the neck down, and she could not breathe without mechanical help; at night, her iron lung breathed for her.

Unexpectedly, the electricity had just gone off, she realized, and her backup generator had not switched on. With no power, her telephone and intercom would not work either. She was physically incapable of yelling loud enough to call her sister and brother-in-law, who were sleeping upstairs.

In the night's stillness, Murphy told herself to stay calm. To take in oxygen, she tried "frog breathing," using her tongue and the back of her throat to push small gulps of air into her lungs. Normally, she could keep herself alive that way for hours. But that night, with her neck tightly bound so the iron lung would work, just half an hour of frog breathing exhausted her.

Anxiously, she searched her mind for a way to save herself. She thought of Rosie, her rust-colored, floppy-eared Doberman–Labrador retriever mutt, sleeping on the sofa in the next room. Rosie was solicitous and loving: Once when Murphy had asked her for kisses, the dog had licked her face and, in the process, had removed three mosquitoes that the woman herself was unable to swat.

She softly called Rosie, and the dog got up from the sofa and ran to her. From the fright in the woman's voice—and the silence of the iron lung, intercom, and telephone—Rosie perceived that Murphy was in trouble. The dog obviously wanted to help. She barked so urgently that Murphy's brother-in-law took only one minute to rush downstairs and connect Murphy's iron lung to batteries.

Rosie sat beside Murphy until the woman felt reassured and safe again. Then the dog returned to her sofa, still close enough to respond if Murphy needed her again.

EVE, a 104-pound rottweiler, stared intently out the windshield as her owner, Cathy Vaughn, drove along Interstate 65 in Indiana. Suddenly, thick smoke billowed through the van. Vaughn, who was paralyzed from the waist down, pulled to the side of the highway and reached back for her wheelchair, so that she could escape. But Eve must have realized that Vaughn did not have time to save herself.

The rottweiler grabbed Vaughn's leg and dragged her twenty feet from the van, only seconds before it burst into flames. Although Vaughn got only a few bruised ribs from the dragging, Eve severely burned her paws in the blaze. She had never been taught to be a service dog; she'd never even had obedience training.

LINK HILL, an amateur prospector, had finished panning for gold at the North Fork of California's Yuba River. He climbed onto a rock to get a gas can, slipped, and tumbled into the rushing water. The water was so rough and deep that he could not save himself. Neither could he shout for help—he was deaf and mute.

Rapids swept him downstream toward Lillian McDermott and her adolescent, 110-pound Newfoundland, Boo, who were playing near the shore. McDermott threw the dog a stick. On a forty-foot leash, he charged through the water in pursuit. Looking pleased with himself, he pranced back to McDermott with the stick in his mouth. She threw it again.

As the current carried Hill closer, Boo dropped his stick. Although seconds earlier, he'd been ecstatic about the game, the dog seemed suddenly disinterested. He looked back and forth from McDermott to the river several times. Curious, she leaned down to see what had attracted his attention: At first glance, a log appeared to be rolling through the water.

Looking agitated, Boo started to bark.

"It's all right." McDermott tried to soothe him.

The dog continued barking.

McDermott scanned the river again and saw that the "log" was not a log at all. An arm reached out of the water. A hand clutched a gas can. But as soon as Link's entire body surfaced, the white water pulled him under again.

Boo looked at McDermott; the expression on his face begged her to let him off the leash. She understood what he was asking. After she released him, he dashed into the water and swam toward Link. All McDermott could see of her dog was just a few inches of his bushy, black tail.

When Boo reached Link, the dog seized the man's wrist gently in his mouth; Link held onto Boo's collar with his free hand. The dog tugged and pulled Link through the dangerous rapids back to shore and saved the deaf-mute man from drowning.

As a little girl, Kara Wilson loved to gallop her horse through the sagebrush on her family's cattle ranch in Fossil, Oregon. Her most cherished dream was to become a rodeo barrel racer. Yet at age seven, she was bitten by a tick and contracted Lyme disease. By age nine, she was so severely disabled that she had to use a wheelchair. Ever being able to ride again seemed inconceivable.

Nevertheless, she wanted so desperately to go horseback riding that on days when she felt relatively well, her father sat her on pillows in front of his saddle and rode with her around the ranch. Sometimes the horse's rocking motion caused so much pain that tears streamed down her cheeks, but she gritted her teeth and endured the discomfort.

When Kara was sixteen, a man in Washington read a magazine article about her and learned of her dream to ride a horse alone. He was certain that he had the perfect horse to give her: Dan, a small sorrel gelding, who was sensitive, reliable, and gentle. After Dan came to her family's ranch, Kara bought a special saddle, so she could rest her legs on top of the pommel and her feet on either side of Dan's neck. Two seat belts held her legs and hips in place.

One Memorial Day, she perched in this precarious position on Dan's back and rode around the rodeo ring—alone for the first time. Filled with new hope about her life, Kara was jubilant. Dan undoubtedly sensed how fragile she was; he turned his head around again and again to look at her, as if he were making sure she was safe.

Kara and Dan were eventually able to compete in barrel racing at her high school's rodeos. The horse's attentiveness to her disability gave her the chance to fulfill her childhood dream.

MASSIVE, POWERFUL HORSES, such as Dan—as well as other kinds of animals—can be so considerate and kind to a disabled person that they're often used as physical therapists for improving strength, coordination, and balance. Although the animals can be trained to do their job efficiently, no one can teach them to feel compassion. That must come from their hearts.

• One afternoon I went to observe Java, a shiny mahogany mare who'd been rescued, starving and abused, and then given to the National Center for Equine Facilitated Therapy in Woodside, California. The horse's head was held down by a woman walking behind her and holding the reins. Java looked as if she were plowing a field as she plodded around a covered arena with Heather, a seven-year-old child with cerebral palsy, on her back. Occasionally, the therapists made Java stop so they could readjust Heather's position. Although horses supposedly hate standing still and can be very begrudging and sullen about it, Java was not. Always patient and conscientious, she remained as motionless as concrete until she was told to walk again.

At the end of the session, the therapists held Heather up to tell Java good-bye. Instead of roughly nudging her, the horse slowly inched her nose toward Heather and rested it gently under her hand. Java also restrained her natural urge to take a giant, reckless chomp out of the apple Heather offered her. Careful not to frighten the child, Java took only a delicate nibble. Undoubtedly, she was aware of Heather's fragile condition.

• In *Dolphin Society,* Linda Erb told the story of AJ, a dolphin at Florida's Dolphin Research Center. One afternoon AJ worked with Lindley, a thirty-year-old man who had cerebral palsy. After Lindley got out of his wheelchair into the pool, AJ swam up to him very slowly so as not to frighten him, then offered his .orsal fin to take Lindley for a swim. Because the man's illness made his fingers curl uncontrollably toward his palms, he could not grasp the fin. AJ seemed to understand. The dolphin waited as if nothing mattered more to him than helping. Lindley rested his head on AJ's side and breathed rapidly in order to relax his hand enough to open it.

When Lindley finally was able to grab the fin, AJ didn't flinch. With exquisite sensitivity—clearly conscious of his fragile charge—the dolphin glided across the pool. Lindley smiled with such pleasure that a light seemed to shine from his face.

———

THE SUMMER of 1995 was miserable for Ray and Carol Steiner. Record-breaking heat for four months in Bowling Green, Ohio, forced them to close every window in their house and stay inside with air-conditioning.

What made their situation even worse is that Ray was incapacitated from a triple-bypass operation, and Carol was hobbling around on crutches after recent surgery on her foot. When she and Ray began suffering memory loss, high blood pressure, headaches, and dizziness, their doctor assumed that they just needed time to recover from the operations. Their sleeping nineteen hours a day was another symptom that would pass, he said.

In the mornings their cat, Ringo, joined them for naps, but he mostly spent the sultry days hiding in the flower bed watching hummingbirds. He was a twenty-six-pound red tabby Manx, a giant the size of a bobcat yet, despite originally being feral, not nearly as fierce. He could get huffy at times, though. When Carol gave piano lessons and locked him in the kitchen, he pounded the glass doors with his huge paws to show his resentment. He never meowed; instead, he expressed his feelings by drumming, like his namesake Ringo Starr.

One hot Saturday morning, Ringo, as usual, ate his breakfast, patrolled the yard, and returned to the house. Carol let him in and clumped on crutches back to her hospital bed in the living room, where Ray was napping on the sofa. Instead of joining the couple in their daily nap, Ringo hung around the entry hall.

Just as Carol got settled in bed, she heard a WHAM! Looking into the hall, she saw Ringo standing by the front door, apparently desperate to go out. He was certainly being inconsiderate, she thought. After breakfast, he always took a nap. Now he expected a disabled woman to do his bidding.

Carol wobbled across the living room again and opened the front door. But Ringo, instead of going outside, put his foot on the threshold and froze.

208 • *Sensitivity to Disability*

"Go on," Carol insisted.

Ringo stood there like a marble statue.

Carol gently nudged him with her crutch. "Go!"

He refused to budge.

"All right, Ringo." Carol impatiently pulled him inside and closed the door; her crutches dug into her armpits as she made her way back to bed.

Ringo followed but then walked to the entry hall again. He backed up ten feet, took a flying leap, and charged. Another WHAM! His hips and shoulders crashed against the door.

The cat was again demanding to be let out. "I'm going to kill you, Ringo," Carol said.

Disgruntled, she got up and re-opened the front door. Ringo stepped outside, but only part way. Planting his rear legs in the hall and his front legs on the porch, he balked and would go no farther.

"Ringo!" Carol threatened. If her frustration had had heat, his fur would have singed. "You *are* going out. Now."

The tabby leaned his head back and looked at her expectantly. For the first time since she'd brought him home as a tiny kitten three years ago, he meowed. His meow was not delicate or pianissimo; it was so loud and raucous and throaty that it resonated through the hall. With defiance, he placed his left hind paw on the threshold, so Carol could not shut him out or close the door.

"What's *wrong* with you?"

Ringo answered with a commanding stare. His expression insisted that Carol follow him outside.

"You're just going to lead me to a dead mouse," she told him. "Why do you have to cause so much trouble when I can hardly get around?"

Still, his forehead was creased with such obvious worry that she felt compelled to find out what was distressing him.

"I'm going outside," she called to Ray, who was sound asleep and did not answer.

Weak and dizzy, Carol slowly made her way out the door and into the backyard. Ringo, she was surprised to see, seemed to understand her difficulty on crutches. He stayed out of her way to avoid tripping her, but walked close enough to seem solicitous. After a few steps, he stopped, stared up at her, and waited for her to catch up before he moved on. Gradually, he led her to the side of the house.

"This dead animal you've caught for me is going to be a real doozy," Carol said.

However, there was no dead animal near the gas meter, where Ringo stopped. He scratched lightly in the lava rock, which had been spread over hard clay around the meter. When Carol did nothing but stand and watch him, he dug so furiously that his paws bled. He stopped, raised his head, and looked back at Carol as if he were desperate to communicate with her. Then he curled his lip.

Carol had learned from her father, a chemist, that cats curl their lips when they analyze scents; a special organ in the roof of the mouth transmits information to the brain about the scent's chemistry. Carol was certain that Ringo was smelling something that disgusted him. And he had brought her there to smell it, too.

She swung her crutch around, so she could lean down toward him and sniff. Natural gas blew at her with the force of wind.

"Oh, my God!" She screamed for Ray. "We're going to explode!"

With crutches flying, Carol hauled herself back to the house. When she opened the back door, Ringo pressed his body against it and kept it from slamming against her. She hobbled inside.

"We've got a gas leak!" Carol yelled to Ray.

"Well, okay," he mumbled. Leaking gas, not weakness from surgery, had been causing his and Carol's wooziness and disabling them for weeks. His mind was so dazed that this alarming insight failed to register on him with any emotional impact at all. He went back to sleep.

Carol called the Columbia Gas Company and hurried out to the yard with Ringo to wait for the service technician. When he arrived, he immediately covered the meter with detergent.

"If there's a gas leak, it'll make a bubble in the soap," he explained.

No bubble appeared. He moved a hand-held meter around the gas meter, but nothing registered.

"Mrs. Steiner, there's nothing to worry about," he reassured her.

Carol didn't believe him. "Will you bring your meter over to where the cat is?" She pointed to Ringo, sitting exactly where he'd clawed into the lava rock.

Ringo moved to make room for the serviceman. When the man held his meter over the spot, the meter wailed like a siren. He ran back to his truck for another instrument. The needle on its dial shot to the highest reading to indicate escaping gas.

"Your house is about to blow up!" he shouted.

A cold sweat beaded on Carol's forehead as he turned off the gas.

Carol and Ray kept it off for the rest of the weekend and aired out the house—and cleared their heads. But when a plumber arrived on Monday, he dug below the gas meter and claimed that there had never been a leak at all.

"The pipe is fine," he insisted.

Carol pointed to the spot Ringo had shown her. "Try digging there."

Exactly there the plumber found the fitting that connected the Steiner's gas meter to the neighborhood's main gas line. The fitting was split and rusty, and gas had been pouring out of it.

That night Carol and Ray, feeling well for the first time in weeks, watched television in the family room. As Ringo cuddled up between them, Carol ran her hand over the bull's-eye rings of fur on his flanks.

"You know, this cat saved our lives," she said.

"The neighbors' lives, too," Ray pointed out.

Since the Steiner's gas pipe was connected to the pipes of six other houses, they could have all exploded simultaneously. Ringo's detecting the leak and insisting that Carol follow him had saved twenty-two people.

CHAPTER NINETEEN

A BLESSING *to* THEIR OWN KIND

A CAT IN Iowa had a litter of kittens, and the couple she lived with found homes for all but one. A few weeks later the mother cat and her kitten disappeared. The couple's long and frantic search for them proved fruitless.

Just as the couple had given up hope of ever seeing their cat and her kitten again, the mother appeared, alone. She acted as if she had never been gone or even had a litter at all. After eating her dinner, she curled up on the sofa and fell asleep, just as she'd always done.

The couple, though thrilled that she'd come home again, was baffled about where she'd been. And what had happened to her kitten? They worried endlessly about it until the mystery was solved one afternoon, when they took a walk and the mother cat came along.

As they passed a house many blocks from theirs, a woman rushed outside.

She pointed at the cat. "Is she yours?"

Yes, she was, the couple said.

"She brought a kitten here a few weeks ago. She made such a fuss that I let them in."

Grasping the kitten in her mouth, the mother cat had jumped onto the woman's bed and deposited her progeny on the pillow. She'd stayed with the kitten for a short while, then vanished.

"I guess she figured she'd found a good home for her baby," the woman said. "She knew she could leave."

Evidently forgiving the mother cat for her hasty departure, the woman stooped down and petted her. "She still comes back once in a while to visit the kitten."

———

FIVE KITTENS cried in terror as fire blazed out of a vacant Brooklyn building early one morning. The kittens' mother, dashing in and out of the flames, picked her babies up one at a time and carried them a few feet out of the building. When they were safe, she began transporting them again, one by one, to a sheltered spot across the street.

Fireman David Gianelli found the cat after she'd rescued just two of the kittens. Her paws were severely burned; her eyes were blistered shut. Because of the red patches of skin showing through her scorched fur, she was named Scarlett.

Despite her injuries, the cat's maternal concern was obvious: When someone placed her in a basket with her kittens again, she could not see to make certain they were all there—so she counted by touching each one with her charred nose.

ANIMALS WATCHING out for their own babies may not be so surprising; people might chalk up the creatures' attentiveness not to compassion, but to maternal instinct. Yet many animals have also watched over others who have no genetic link to them. They simply offer kindness without expecting anything in return.

Just before my friend Joe Backus died of cancer in Honolulu, he asked if I'd take care of Yin, his Siamese cat. Of course, I promised, and I considered my stewardship of Yin to be a sacred trust. I assured Joe that I would see her through to the end.

The cat was twenty-two years old, deaf, crotchety, and ill-mannered. In all of her long years, she'd never figured out how to use a litter box. Long before Joe's death, she'd given up grooming herself, rubbing against people's ankles, and greeting visitors with civility. Like an arthritic gargoyle, she lurked on top of Joe's refrigerator and closet shelves.

After his death, I flew to Hawaii to claim her. I bought her a little carrying case and took her to the vet for a tranquilizer to calm her during the long trans-Pacific flight back to my house. The vet, a muscular, gray-haired woman who should have been barking orders at Marine recruits, dragged Yin out of the case.

In rebellion, she scraped her toenails, too old to retract, against the case's plastic.

The vet placed Yin on a steel exam table and thumped on her ribs and pelvis, which jutted from beneath her matted, unkempt fur. Then, as if the vet were pushing apart a snapdragon, she forced Yin's mouth open and exposed her few remaining ancient teeth.

Yin was not amused. She let out a raucous squawk of protest. I cringed, but the vet seemed unconcerned.

"You think you're gonna fly with this cat?"

"I promised my friend I'd take care of her."

"Let me tell you. She's an old lady. You should put her down."

"I could never do that."

The vet listed all the logical reasons why Yin was better off dead than with me. At such an advanced age, she'd never adapt to new surroundings. She was too geriatric to take care of herself. She'd be lonely, confused, and upset—not to mention depressed. She'd surely die within a week after coming to my house.

I was not sure whether the vet was trying to test my resolve about keeping Yin or if she really believed that I should agree to euthanize the cat. I still refused. Trying not to show my annoyance at the woman, I packed Yin back into her carrying case, paid for her tranquilizer, and went to the airport.

Watching her carrying case move down the baggage conveyor onto our flight made my heart squeeze with sadness. As Yin peered out from behind the door's metal bars, I worried that perhaps the vet had been right.

Maybe the little bed I'd made for Yin out of Joe's flannel shirts would not keep her warm. Maybe her water would spill on her and freeze her. Maybe the tranquilizer wouldn't work, the high altitude would make her sick, the taking off and landing would frighten her.

The "maybes" gnawed on me the entire trip home until I opened Yin's case and set her free. She was anything but happy. From her seven hours' confinement, her fur was askew; it stuck out from her body like bristles from a bottle brush. She went immediately to my guest room and urinated on the baseboards.

Initially, all she did was stare into space, a sign of her despair, perhaps, or a defense against bewilderment. Then, for the next few days, she wandered from room to room and squawked mournfully, as if she were searching for Joe or for something familiar. She seemed to be grieving.

Adding to Yin's adjustment problem was the hostility of my tabby, Tigger, who, until Yin's arrival, had been a pampered, only cat. Tigger took one look at Yin, arched her back, and fluffed up her fur to look large and fierce. Then Tigger hissed as if her hiss were only a prelude to a more vicious assault. The fur stood erect along her spine; an electric current seemed to be passing through it.

But in spite of her display of aggression, I think Tigger realized that fighting Yin would be futile; the ancient cat was too feeble to defend herself. Yin didn't get along with my dogs either. They trailed her, rudely sniffed her, and put my house in an uproar for several weeks.

I, of course, worried constantly. Had the vet been right? Should I have let her put Yin down? Everything inside me had insisted, "Absolutely not," but a niggling doubt kept whispering "Maybe."

One morning seemed to be the turning point. I went into my office. The sun was shining through the matchstick blinds onto the sofa and warming it with a soft, diffused light. Yin and Tigger were cuddled up together among my needlepoint pillows. Overnight, Tigger seemed to have taken Yin on as her personal ward.

Tigger had curled her body around Yin's shoulders and, with great gentleness, was giving Yin a bath. As Tigger worked her rough, pink tongue over Yin's fur, she slowly turned it from pearl gray to an oyster white that shimmered in the sunshine. For the first time since I'd brought Yin home, she was purring. And clean.

She lived, with Tigger's help, to the age of twenty-five.

AUTOMOBILES, the nemesis of creatures, cause disasters that can draw as much compassion from animals as they do from people who aid the victims of a wreck.

· Conan, a malamute-wolf mix, often roamed the streets in Randolph, Vermont, and visited Margo, a fluffy Samoyed. Though Margo was usually confined to Marjorie Ryerson's yard, the dog got loose one day and joined Conan for a walk. But the Samoyed was not street-smart. As a car sped directly toward her, she stood in the middle of the road and did not have the sense to run away. Conan rushed over and pushed her to the curb but got hit by the car himself. Although his leg was badly injured, he'd managed to keep Margo safe.

• A stray male German shepherd found a female Doberman pinscher lying in the gutter of a busy Los Angeles street. She was unable to get up because a car had hit her. As more cars whizzed by, the shepherd lay down and covered her with his body. Estella Dvorin, who called for help for the dogs, believed that the shepherd was trying to keep the Doberman from being hit a second time. She was so badly injured that she had to be put down. Los Angeles's Department of Animal Protection auctioned off the stray male shepherd to a man who greatly respected the dog's compassion and paid one thousand dollars for him.

———

As ANNE URBANOS sorted laundry one morning, her dog Minnie jumped up from her sleeping spot at the open front door and barreled down the hall toward the woman. Barking, Minnie leaped on the bed, looked anxiously out the window, and ran back to Urbanos.

She got Minnie's message. "All right. All right. I'm coming." Not knowing what to expect, Urbanos went to the front door.

A gray cat, evidently hit by a car, was lying on the street in front of the house. Since Urbanos had let out her gray tabby Crockett only a few minutes earlier, she was terrified that he might be the cat in the street.

As she ran outside with a feeling of dread, Crockett suddenly appeared from under a bush. Relieved but still concerned about the other cat, Urbanos walked over to see it. Crockett accompanied her and began butting his head against the motionless animal. When it did not move, he looked up at Urbanos and meowed pitifully, as if he were asking her to help. He tried to push the cat with his paws out of the way of passing cars, then grasped its tail in his mouth and dragged the dead creature to the side of the street.

A neighbor, who hurried out of her house to assist Urbanos, said that she had often seen Crockett and the other cat sunning themselves together. "Crockett's guarding the kitty," she said sadly.

Next to the curb, Crockett lay down beside his friend and refused to leave even when Urbanos called him. Crockett stayed with the cat's body until someone took it away.

───────

IN THE middle of a summer night, Tuffy, a black standard poodle, barked and clawed at Arthur Martin's back door. Startled, he opened his eyes. Usually Tuffy and his other dog, Sandy, a nineteen-year-old terrier, wandered around his Medford, Oregon, farm at night and never bothered him. What could be the matter?

Martin got out of bed, went downstairs to the back door and looked outside. Tuffy, clearly upset, barked at him and ran toward the fields, then stopped and glanced back. Martin could tell that Tuffy was asking him to follow. Since Sandy appeared to be missing, Martin worried that something had happened to him.

Martin got a flashlight, hurried outdoors, and trailed Tuffy a quarter of a mile to an irrigation ditch at the far end of his property. When he shone his light into the water, all that he could see was Sandy's nose. Certain that his dog had drowned, Martin bent down and looked closer. The old terrier was standing on his hind legs and bracing himself with his front legs against the cement wall of the ditch. Miraculously—for who knows how many hours—Sandy had balanced himself there to stay alive.

As Tuffy whimpered in sympathy, Martin pulled the older dog out of the water, carried him home, and dried him off. Sandy, too weak to walk after his ordeal, spent the night on a rug in the house. Tuffy, who was not allowed inside, guarded Sandy through the back-door screen until morning. Finally, Tuffy ended his vigil and lay down, exhausted. His rescue completed, at last he could sleep.

———

RANGER, a German shepherd, began barking constantly—hour after hour, day after day—beside an old camper shell in Espanola, New Mexico. Whenever he stopped making noise, he disappeared under the shell. A neighbor watched him come out, take a mouthful of snow, and then return to the shell, again and again. Puzzled by his behavior but sorry for him because he was surely hungry and distressed, she gave him canned tuna in a plastic cup. Instead of eating the tuna, he carried the cup in his teeth and crawled under the camper shell.

More than a week later, someone finally went over to see what all the barking and the mouthfuls of snow were about. A stray female mutt was caught in a coyote trap; her leg was crushed. In subzero weather, Ranger had been taking care of her. Though she was in pain, she was still alive, and her leg eventually healed.

DUKE WAS a nearly perfect dog, according to Dee and Brett Anderson of Wheatfield, Kansas. Part German shepherd and part Labrador retriever, he was black with a handsome white chest and brown paws. He played gently with small children, protected the Andersons' house, and chased rabbits from the garden. Although he suffered from painful arthritis, he was cheerful and loving.

But he had one flaw: He was fiercely possessive of his food. When the Andersons answered a newspaper ad and brought home another pup, whom they named Midnight and who looked just like Duke, the older dog jealously guarded his kibble and would not let Midnight come anywhere near it. Sometimes he even chased Midnight away from his *own* bowl and raided his puppy chow.

"You let Midnight eat. Leave him alone," Dee often scolded Duke.

If Dee loomed over him long enough, he would slink away from Midnight's bowl and let the pup eat in peace.

At Christmas, six weeks after Midnight had come to live with the Andersons, he disappeared. Imagining that the puppy had frozen to death in the snow, they searched their property, asked neighbors if they'd seen him, and checked nearby roads and ditches for his body. Since the Andersons lived near a popular Christmas-tree farm, they were afraid that a customer had run over Midnight or carted him away. No matter how hard they searched or how many people they asked about their pup, Brett and Dee could find no trace of him.

"Where's the puppy?" Dee kept asking Duke. "Did someone steal Midnight?"

Duke obviously could not answer, but he tried. Every day he barked and barked in the snowy woods next to their house.

Brett told Dee that Duke was probably just chasing rabbits.

They told each other that they should be glad they hadn't found Midnight's body. Perhaps he was still alive. If he didn't turn up in a week, they'd put an ad in the paper and see if someone had found him. In the meantime, if he were just out roaming, they'd give him a chance to find his way home.

Never had a week passed so slowly.

A few days after Christmas, Brett walked into the woods and heard agitated barking that surely must be his neighbor's dog, he thought. The dog sounded so desperate that Brett, thinking it needed help, followed the barks farther into the woods.

He found Midnight, nearly frozen to death and hanging by his hind paws from a barbed-wire fence. The wire had twisted around him so tightly that each time he'd tried to squirm free, it had cut deeper into his flesh. The blood had not been able to circulate in one of his paws; it had frozen as solidly as a block of ice.

In spite of his pain, Midnight squealed with happiness to see Brett. He could hardly hold the pup still enough to free him as he wriggled and licked Brett with excitement. When Brett carried the pup home, Duke was also ecstatic. Dee steeled herself to keep from crying as she thawed Midnight's frozen paw in cool water. She took him to the vet, and his leg was amputated.

Yet just two days later, when Midnight came home, he jumped out of the car and trotted into the house as if he still had four legs. Duke seemed overjoyed to see him and sniffed him carefully to examine his wound, then curled up with him to keep him warm.

"How did Midnight ever survive?" Brett wondered aloud to Dee.

"I don't know."

"The vet said it was a miracle."

Curious about how that miracle had happened, Brett walked back to the tangled fence where he'd discovered Midnight.

Beneath the fence, as far as the puppy had been able to reach with his front paws, he'd scratched away the snow and dug down to the frozen grass for nourishment and liquid. And next to the fence was a ham bone, licked clean, without a speck of meat left on it.

Dee's mother had given Duke that very ham bone, covered with meat, after Christmas dinner. Apparently, Duke had limped through the snow on his sore, arthritic legs and had taken the bone to Midnight, along with other table scraps when he could get them. Duke had overcome being possessive of food and had shared all he had with the hungry puppy. For nearly a week, Duke had kept Midnight alive in the sleet and snow.

DUKE'S VETERINARIAN, Kirk Smith, claimed that Duke had brought the ham bone to Midnight because Duke considered the pup a member of his canine pack. "Pack animals take care of their own," Smith explained.

Indeed. But pack animals can take care of others who are not "their own" and who belong to an entirely different species. Animals who have no connection at all to the bonding of a pack have also been known to do the same.

• Early one morning Buddy, a collie who belonged to Matthew Crinkley in Budd Lake, New Jersey, watched his barn burst into flames. The dog ran inside to save the seventy pregnant goats that were trapped there. He pushed the goats, nipped at their feet, and herded them out. In spite of his burned paws and a nose injured by smoke inhalation, Buddy tried to wake Crinkley by barking frantically. Crinkley rushed to his window to see the barn's walls and roof slam to the ground in a shower of sparks.

• Spuds, a dalmatian who was unfairly called a dunce by his South Carolina family, sat in the kitchen and watched Dirk Tanis pour oil into a pan to make french fries. Because the oil seemed to be taking a long time to heat and Tanis felt tired from work, he decided to rest on the living room sofa. Soon he fell asleep. A few minutes later, he was jolted awake by teeth biting into his hand.

Spuds, a true fire-house dog, seemed determined to wake him. Tanis jumped off the sofa to see smoke and flames leaping from the skillet oil to the kitchen ceiling. He ran to the stove, turned off the burner, and hurried over to a neighbor's to call for help. But Spuds did not escape with him. Instead, he searched for Gizmo, the family's five-month-old kitten. Spuds carefully picked her up by the scruff of the neck and carried her outside.

• Cream Dee, an English cow described by Paul Simons in *Pet Heroes*, wandered away from her herd and began hovering around a badger hole. The farmer she belonged to, Malcolm Dyer, had been searching five days for his Jack Russell terrier and noticed the cow standing alone, her head lowered to the ground. When he walked over to investigate, he heard whimpers from inside the badger hole. He dug into it and found his terrier trapped inside, disheveled and stressed but still alive.

· Amber, an Abyssinian cat whose story was told in *Cat Fancy*, lived with a woman and her tank of tropical fish. The cat seemed to enjoy watching the fish under the light of the aquarium. But one evening she meowed and meowed so plaintively that the woman came to see what was so upsetting. A fish had jumped through a hole in the tank's cover and was flopping around on the floor. After the woman scooped up the fish and put it back into the water, Amber stopped crying. She settled down again to gaze at the fish.

CAMEO, a black-and-white cat, was not exactly pleased when Ed and Toni Eames adopted her in Fresno, California. All her life, she'd lived with an elderly woman as a privileged "only" cat. Now she had to share a house with two other cats and two lumbering golden retrievers.

Initially, Cameo was terrified of the animals whose territory she had invaded, and she hid behind the stove or on a closet shelf. Then she slowly learned to tolerate the cats and realized that her hissing scared away the dogs. As she gradually became more confident, she joined the family but remained independent and aloof. Cameo always turned her back on Ivy, one of the golden retrievers, with extreme indifference. For years she and Ivy refused to acknowledge each other's presence in the house.

Then Ivy was diagnosed with cardiomyopathy, and she eventually became so sick that she refused to eat, a sure sign that she was no longer interested in living. Toni marshaled all her strength, called her veterinarian, and asked him to come and put Ivy down at home. By the time Toni hung up the phone, her face was wet with tears.

Cameo, usually so remote, jumped into her arms and nuzzled her as if she wanted to comfort her. When the vet arrived and Toni sat on the floor with Ivy, Cameo, purring, walked back and forth between them. Suddenly she stopped in front of Ivy. For the first time in all her years of living with the dog, Cameo licked her tired, wizened face, as if she were saying a final, loving good-bye.

As the vet gave Ivy the injection to free her from her old, sick body, Cameo lay facing her and purring, as if she wanted to send Ivy off with care and compassion. Cameo comforted Ivy through the dog's last breath.

———

MICHELLE AND DICK Knutson of Appleton, Wisconsin, noticed that their dog Tiffany kept disappearing for hours in a field behind their house. They had no explanation for her odd behavior until they looked outside one morning and saw Tiffany leading six tiny kittens across the lawn up to the doorstep. On wobbly legs, the kittens meowed and clamored for food.

The Knutsons were certain that Tiffany had been tending the kittens in the field, where their mother had either abandoned them or died. Now Tiffany continued to care for them in her dog house. At mealtimes, she rounded them up and herded them to the Knutson's kitchen, where Michelle fed them from a bottle, then progressed to baby cereal. Because of Tiffany's concern, the kittens lived.

Animals frequently watch after other animals' babies; as in the case of Tiffany and her kittens, those babies are not necessarily members of the same species. I read about a dog who raised possums and cats who fostered-parented squirrels, hedgehogs, rabbits, and a sparrow. Occasionally, the foster mothers' intense involvement with their adopted brood somehow activates their hormonal system, and they begin to lactate, so they can nurse.

Sometimes the "mothers" are even male, as Yvonne Roberts described in *Animal Heroes.* Pedro, a Great Pyrenees in England, adopted and raised an orphaned lamb. And Sidney, a mutt rescued from the streets and taken to an animal shelter, looked after four tiny orphaned hedgehogs. When the staff placed them by a radiator to keep them warm, Sidney wandered over, sniffed them, curled up beside them—and stayed to "mother" them for several weeks.

———

GRIZ, a hulking 650-pound grizzly bear, rooted around in his lunch at Wildlife Images, an animal rehabilitation center near Grants Pass, Oregon. In Griz's five-gallon feed bucket were apples, oranges, vegetables, kibble, chicken, and road-kill venison—a feast he was

gobbling up with such pleasure that he did not notice a six-week-old, orange tabby kitten clamber under the fence into his pen.

The kitten, which weighed just over half a pound, had recently been dumped at the shelter and was forlorn and hungry. He cautiously stepped closer to Griz, sat down beside him, and meowed to ask for food.

As Griz looked up from his lunch and contemplated the tiny creature, Dave Siddons, the shelter's founder, watched in alarm. "Oh, God!" he thought. "Griz is going to eat that kitten!"

But Siddons would never be able to reach the kitten in time. At any moment, Griz would undoubtedly swat him and kill him for an extra bite of lunch. Siddons wished that bears were not omnivores.

Although Griz was an extremely sweet-natured animal, he could be just as violent as any bear when hunting for food. A train had slammed into him and damaged his brain when, as a cub, he'd foraged for spilled grain on a Montana railroad track. A Native American tribe had crated him up and sent him, unconscious, to Siddons, who, along with his staff, had nursed and hand-fed Griz for weeks. After that coddling, the bear was too tame and gentle to survive in the wild.

Nevertheless, the bear was not so gentle that he would stop himself from killing the kitten. With gritted teeth, Siddons braced himself for a tragedy.

Griz looked down at the tabby and did nothing. Then he picked a chicken wing out of his pile of food, pulled off a little meat, and set it on the ground beside his paw for the kitten. The tiny creature pounced on the food and devoured it. Griz fed him a few more scraps.

Later that day, the kitten curled up on the bear's chest, in the crook of his arm, and napped with him. From then on, even after the kitten grew up and had acquired the name "Cat," Griz shared his food with him. They played together like the best of friends. Cat would conceal himself behind the pine trees in the bear's one-acre pen, then leap out and swat Griz's nose. The bear often carried Cat around in his mouth or let Cat ride on his back. Sometimes Griz licked Cat until he was clean, and at night they even slept together.

An unlikely friendship? Indeed. But proof that compassion may be the first step for animals—and humans—to live in harmony.

CHAPTER TWENTY

THE ULTIMATE
SACRIFICE

ANIMALS ARE often so concerned with helping someone in need that they lose all regard for their own well-being. Occasionally, they pay for their compassion.

• Zorro, a German shepherd–wolf mix, was hiking in the Sierras with Mark Cooper of Orangeville, California, when Cooper slipped, fell eighty-five feet down a steep ravine, and landed, unconscious, in a whirlpool. Zorro bolted down to him and tugged him out of the water and up a rocky slope. When Cooper regained consciousness, a friend who had come along on the hike went for help. That night, as the temperature dropped, Zorro slept on top of Cooper to keep him warm.

The next day rescuers arrived for Cooper in a helicopter, but they had to leave Zorro behind. The dog loyally settled down beside Cooper's backpack. *Days later*, two Sierra Club volunteers found him, starving and freezing, still huddled by Cooper's belongings. The dog's own suffering could not make him leave the backpack he thought he should protect—or the place where he hoped Cooper would return.

• Top, a Great Dane belonging to Axel Patzwaldt in Los Angeles, was walking with a young girl one afternoon when she started to cross the street without looking for oncoming cars. A large truck rumbled toward her. Top barked at it, jumped in front of the girl, and pushed her out of its path. Luckily, the girl was safe, but the truck hit the dog and shattered his ribs and right hind leg.

A veterinarian set Top's leg in a cast, but even after the cast was removed seven weeks later, he limped around in constant pain. One afternoon he hobbled to the swimming pool in Patzwaldt's apartment building, then, dripping, ran back as fast as he could *in spite of the pain.* Top barked, basso forte, until Patzwaldt followed him to the pool. A two-year-old boy lay blue and lifeless at the bottom.

After a long stay in the hospital and complicated medical care, the boy was saved. Top had a more difficult recovery. His ribs, broken by the truck two months earlier, became so severely infected that he had to undergo surgery. For being a hero, he had to limp in pain for the rest of his life.

• Woodie, a collie-mix, trotted along the trail of a nature reserve near Cleveland with Rae Anne Knitter and her fiancé, Ray Thomas.

"Wait here. I'll be back in a minute," Thomas said. "I want to take a photo from that cliff."

Heading toward the precipice, Thomas disappeared over a hill. Knitter waited patiently for him, but Woodie sensed that the man was in trouble, even though he was out of her sight. She tugged on her leash so insistently that Knitter finally let her loose and chased her uphill. At the top, Knitter looked into the ravine and saw Thomas lying, facedown and unconscious, in a river at the base of the cliff. He had fallen eighty feet.

Woodie had already plunged down the eighty-foot drop after Thomas. The dog was desperately nudging his face out of the water. She stopped, barked frantically to Knitter as if asking for help, and went back to rescuing Thomas.

In his fall, he had broken his back and arm in several places, but he eventually recovered. In her brave rescue, Woodie had suffered internal injuries and had broken *both* hips. But her pain had not prevented her from trying to keep Thomas alive in the water. She'd given her all in order to save a person's life.

SPARKY, a blond Labrador retriever, had not had a good start in life. An irresponsible woman in Tullahoma, Tennessee, had bought him as a cuddly pup and then had become distressed at his eating so much and mushrooming into a hulking adolescent. She traded Sparky to a garage mechanic for a used car. The mechanic then gave him to another man, who went on vacation and left the dog with his neighbor, Bo Culbertson.

However, being shunted from place to place for a year and a half apparently had not ruined Sparky. Instead of becoming insecure, the dog was loving and outgoing. In just a few days, Bo grew attached to him.

Sparky's owner came home from his trip and asked Bo, "You want the dog?"

Of course he did. Finally, Sparky had a real home where he belonged and where someone loved and appreciated him.

Sparky seemed to be grateful—and he was always hungry for both affection *and* food. He grew from eighty-five pounds to a strapping one hundred fifty. The dog was supremely loyal to Bo and slept next to him every night. Each morning, they hiked a mile together.

On one of the walks, about four hundred yards from the house, Bo suddenly felt weak and dizzy. The world around him faded to gray, then turned black. Trying to steady himself, he shoved his hand under Sparky's steel choke chain and collapsed on the road.

Sparky realized that something terrible was happening and Bo needed help. But with the man's hand tangled in his choke collar, Sparky could not free himself in order to fetch Bo's wife, Dottie. Trying to walk forward and drag Bo home would not work either because in just a few steps, the choke chain would strangle Sparky.

The dog turned around, so the chain would cut into the base of his skull and not into his throat. With the steel links pressing painfully into his flesh, Sparky *walked backwards* and pulled Bo along the road. Step by agonizing step, the dog kept tugging. His task was nearly impossible, not only because of the steel cutting into him and choking him, but also because of Bo's weighing 227 pounds.

After Sparky dragged Bo two hundred yards, he regained consciousness just enough to realize how painful the dog's efforts to get him home must be. In order to help Sparky, Bo pulled his hand out from under the choke chain and leaned his body across Sparky's back. The dog struggled the last two hundred yards home under Bo's weight—seventy-seven pounds heavier than the dog himself. Just as Dottie came outside to leave for work, she was stunned to see Sparky set Bo down at the front door.

The house was so far from the hospital that Dottie was afraid to wait for an ambulance; she could get Bo there faster if she drove him herself. But Dottie was not strong enough to carry him to the car. Once again, Sparky took Bo on his back. Straining and heaving, the dog carried him to the passenger door, where Dottie rolled him onto the front seat. She sped away and left Sparky behind, exhausted.

At the hospital, doctors discovered that the arteries to Bo's heart were blocked. Immediately he underwent triple-bypass surgery. Due to complications that required two more surgeries, Bo spent three months, close to death, in his hospital bed. For all those months, Sparky waited on Bo's empty bed at home and refused to move except to eat or go out on a leash. When Bo finally did come home and had to spend another year in bed, Sparky lay beside him constantly.

In time, one of the dog's legs became cancerous. Though in the past it had been strong enough to support Bo's weight, now the leg could barely hold up Sparky's body. He had three surgeries, but the cancer spread to his lungs. Bo had to put him down.

Bo's voice still breaks when he admits how much he misses Sparky. The dog's photograph on the wall cannot replace his fur, breath, wagging tail, and gentle presence. As do so many people who have been deeply touched by an animal, Bo hopes to meet Sparky again when he dies.

"If I pray hard enough, Sparky will be with me," he said.

With God, Bo believes, all things are possible— including a reunion with a compassionate dog who sacrificed so much for him.

TIM JONES, a police officer in St. Paul, Minnesota, heard one morning that a friend on the force had been shot and killed. His colleagues had tracked the suspect to a woods and were searching for him.

Despite having the day off, Jones left home in his car to join the search team with Laser, his German shepherd police dog. As usual, Laser rode in the back seat and leaned his head over Jones's shoulder. Quite often, he and the dog worked together up to ten hours a day, a longer time than Jones spent with his wife and two small children. His bond with the dog was so close that they almost seemed to be part of each other.

In the woods, Laser sniffed the ground and led Jones to an ice-fishing shack. Whining, the dog continued to track the scent to a nearby garage. Jones stayed behind and opened the shack's door to look inside. The murderer, waiting in the shadows, instantly shot and killed the policeman.

As Jones fell to the ground, the man ran out of the shack—and straight into Laser, who was tearing back around the garage in order to protect Jones. With overwhelming force, Laser leaped on the murderer, knocked him down, and bit his leg. As the dog hung on with his teeth, the man shot him.

The bullet's impact shattered Laser. He loosened his jaw just long enough for the man to step away. But the dog, though traumatized and bleeding, refused to let the man escape. Laser gathered his strength and grabbed the murderer's leg a second time. Again, the man shot the dog. Laser collapsed but continued to fight for Jones. The shepherd crawled on his belly after the man. A third shot killed him.

Jones and Laser were buried together, just as they'd lived—partners even in death. When the casket was lowered into the ground, Jones's family and friends took solace in knowing that Laser's ashes would always be with him.

THE DAYTON, OHIO, house of George and Charlotte Bradley was too hot and stuffy for Max. Even on chilly winter nights, the black chow mutt insisted on sleeping outdoors, warmed only by his long, silky coat.

Yet for some reason, one New Year's Eve Max's preference changed. Demanding to come in, he whined and pawed the door. Even though the house was as warm as ever, Max refused to go back to the yard.

Was Max sick? George wondered, as he locked up and went to bed. Did Max have some special motive for staying inside?

George, an electrician, had adopted Max as a puppy from people who had decided to give him to the pound. The mutt had repaid George many times over for his last-minute rescue. When George's stepdaughter, Corrie, had recently been sick, for instance, Max had lain for days at the foot of her bed like a vigilant guard.

At 6:30 on that New Year's Day morning, Max seemed just as anxious about George and Charlotte. Growling, the dog backed into their bedroom with his gaze locked on something past the door. He barked and growled again.

"There's a burglar in the house," Charlotte whispered.

As George reached for his gun, he smelled smoke and jumped out of bed. When he turned on the lights, they dimmed—a sure sign that somewhere in the house electrical wires had burned. The popping sound downstairs meant that more wires were shorting.

George ran to the top of the stairs and looked down with apprehension. An orange glow of flames lit up the lowest basement steps. That glow was reflected in the door's white enamel. But the house did not feel especially hot. George decided that he, Charlotte, and Corrie, sleeping in another room upstairs, were not in immediate danger because the fire was contained in the basement. He had plenty of time to call the fire department.

George was wrong. An ironing board had tipped over in the basement, spilled clothes against the water heater, and started a fire. That fire had already slowly burned through the kitchen wall and had loosened the mount of the microwave oven, which had fallen to the stove and broken a gas line. Gas filled the house and could explode at any second. George, however, could not smell the gas because the smoke was so thick.

Feeling safe and in control, he lifted the phone to call the fire department, but the fire had already burned through the telephone lines: The phone was dead. He'd have to call from a neighbor's house.

"Get dressed," George told Charlotte and Corrie. "I'm going to use the phone across the street."

With no thought of impending danger, Charlotte zipped up her jogging suit, and George walked down the stairs toward the front door. He grabbed the knob, paused, then let go of it and looked up at the landing.

"Come on, Max," he called.

Through the balusters, Max gazed at him with baleful eyes. The dog turned around and started back into the bedroom.

"Max!" George tried again.

The usually obedient dog stopped for a second but still defied him—just as he'd refused to leave the family and sleep outside the night before. Max seemed more concerned with protecting Charlotte than with accompanying George; he ignored the flames in the basement and padded into the bedroom.

George reached for the door knob again. Max could come outside later, he decided. He pulled open the door. Air whistled in so forcefully that it yanked the door knob from his hand. Exploding gas blew George fifteen feet into his yard. The kitchen windows shattered, and glass crashed to the floor. Flames swept up the stairs to Charlotte, Corrie, and Max.

For a second, George lay on the ground too stunned to move. From inside the house, Charlotte and Corrie screamed for help. The heat was coming at them and cooking them alive, George realized. He leaped to his feet and started back into the house to save them, but so much heat blasted him that he could not get through the front door.

Inside, Charlotte and Corrie's screams turned to silence. Terrified that the people he loved most were dead, George tore across the street for help. Max could also have easily escaped through the open front door, but he did not. He followed Charlotte to the foot of her bed, where she collapsed. Max stood guard over her.

After George called the fire department, he ran back to the house, climbed a ladder to his bedroom window, and tried to see inside. With the thick smoke and the darkness of the early hour, nothing was visible. He broke the window with a brick; the heat exploded in George's face again and knocked him off the ladder to the ground.

Fire trucks arrived, their sirens screaming.

"You've got to get my family out of there!" George yelled.

"Where did you see them last?"

"In their bedrooms. At the top of the stairs."

One fireman dashed into the house and discovered Corrie, unconscious, on the edge of her bed. Another fireman found Charlotte, also unconscious with seventy percent of her body burned, at the bottom of her bed. Still huddled at her feet was Max, dead from the heat and from smoke inhalation. He'd died in agony. To the very end, he'd protected and comforted Charlotte. She and Corrie lived.

CHAPTER TWENTY-ONE

IN SPITE
of the KINDNESS

WHEN I began researching this book, I interviewed seven animal experts—veterinarians, zoologists, evolutionary biologists, and animal behaviorists. Only one of them agreed with me that animals were capable of compassion.

The basic argument against creatures' caring and showing kindness: Scientific studies have found that animals have no "theory of mind." In other words, they're incapable of putting themselves into our heads and seeing the world as we do. Without that ability, animals cannot understand our troubles, emotions, needs—and, consequently, are incapable of being concerned about them. Says University of Pennsylvania's James Serpell, "There's little evidence that animals feel empathy toward people."

From their research on wildlife, scientists have developed three theories to explain why animal behavior that seems motivated by caring is really motivated by selfishness. With a few twists and turns of logic, some experts also extend these theories to pets.

According to the theory of kin selection, what appear to be kind deeds are simply animals helping out their relatives so as to promote the continuation of their own genes. When monkeys rescue each other in fights or wolves rear each other's young, they aren't really being helpful because they feel altruistic toward the other animals; they're protecting their kin who share their genes and are guaranteeing their own link in evolution. Because pets extend their sense of kin to their human "family," they, like wild animals, instinctively help members of that family and treat close "relatives" preferentially.

The theory of reciprocal altruism suggests that one animal helps another, whether they're related or not, because the helpful one expects to be paid back for its effort. What looks like compassion is really two creatures doling out favors, tit-for-tat. When a zebra cleans fleas off another in its herd, it expects grooming in return. A bat's regurgitating blood into the mouths of bats who have hunted unsuccessfully assures its receiving blood from them on nights when *it* has had bad hunting luck. According to reciprocal altruism, what appears to be animals' caring is merely their calculated way of improving their lives and their chances for survival. Dogs who chase away burglars and pull drowning children out of rivers expect food and shelter in return.

According to the theory of pseudo-reciprocity, when an animal does something that seems kind and beneficial to another, the helpful animal is really preparing the way for an indirect payback that will make its own life better. Evening bats, for example, nurse unrelated babies—but only females, not males. The reason, according to this theory: Only females stay with the colony when they grow up; nursing them means that more bats will be in the colony in the future—and more bats will hunt and bring food home. Just as the nursing bats are looking out for future meals, so are the pets who push their owners out of the paths of oncoming cars or lead them out of burning houses.

Gerald Wilkinson, an associate professor of zoology at the University of Maryland, summed up these three theories' dismissal of animal compassion: As classically defined, he explains, altruism means doing something and getting no return for it in any way. "To my knowledge there is no convincing example in animals where [altruism] occurs," he says, "in spite of occasional cases, which tend to be anecdotal."

All the stories I had collected did not prove animal compassion, Wilkinson and other experts told me, because they *were* anecdotes—trivial, spontaneous, random events signifying nothing. Without a controlled experiment, careful documentation, and quantifiable data that could be analyzed, anecdotes were meaningless.

Experts also told me that I was being anthropomorphic. By concluding from my stories that animals could be compassionate, I was attributing human feelings and qualities to them. Scientists greatly disdain anthropomorphism. Most of them believe that animals are incapable of feeling not only compassion, but any emotion.

"HOW DO you explain the acts of kindness in the stories I've collected?" I asked the experts. A few responses:

• Animals protect and rescue us, not necessarily because they care about us, but because they are driven by instincts, hard-wired into their brains. "Children trigger the maternal instinct in dogs," explains Colorado State Unversity's Temple Grandin. For example, Sheba, who took thirty yellow-jacket stings for a child, or the stray, who wrapped her body around the newborn baby in the alley, were not feeling concern, but rather were following instincts as reflexive as a mother dog taking care of her pup.

According to some scientists, dogs have also transferred their instinctual sense of social order from a dog pack to their human family. In any threatening situation, they automatically try, without thought or feeling, to save the higher-ranking "pack" members in that family. When Bailey fought the bull for Chester Jenkins, in other words, he was mindlessly following an instinct to protect his pack leader, not trying to help someone he loved. So was Bruno when he swallowed the firecracker, or three-legged Tia when she towed the boat to shore.

• Animals warn us of danger because they feel uncomfortable, some researchers argue. Animals run to us, so we can soothe and help *them*. Roc rang the doorbell to alert his owners that the house was on fire because he was agitated by the flames, not because he was concerned that the family would burn. He wanted the fire to stop and the family to calm him.

If he'd been trapped in the house, he'd have alerted his family with the same self-interest, this argument continues. In fires, animals "often go to the person who knows how to open the door and get them out. Coincidentally, they happen to save the person," says Bonnie Beaver, professor at Texas A&M University. In any threatening situation, then, creatures look out for themselves.

• When animals run to "tell" someone that another person is in trouble, they are not trying to get help, one expert explains. They are really just looking for someone to share their excitement about the person's unusual circumstances or behavior. Or they are rushing to find someone who can back them up in the strange situation. According to this argument, Spud ran to the neighbor of the man who'd just had a heart attack, so she could join him in the drama, not help him save someone. Only for reassurance and support, Indian Red, the horse, tried to attract passing cars and Shoo Shoo, the cat, led her owner to the closed door of the woman in seizures.

• Compassion does not motivate animals to cuddle up and seem to comfort people. Rather, the creatures only want the pleasure of being petted and having social contact, some researchers claim. When Sunny, the golden retriever, held Esther Warnes's hand all night after a burglary attempt, Sunny wanted only to be stroked, not to make Warnes feel better.

Or perhaps Warnes's fear had disconcerted Sunny. A person's distress or odd behavior confuses dogs and makes them lie close to the person and act submissive. Says Beaver, "When the animals don't understand what the higher-ranking pack member is trying to tell them [by the unusual behavior], they come up in a submissive way to ask permission to understand." Rosie went to lie in bed with Cheryl Essex after her husband's death only because the dog was confused and trying to understand Essex's tears. Interpreting Rosie's lying next to Essex as comforting her is a mistake.

• Animals risk their life for us because they don't understand danger. "We don't have evidence that animals know they're taking risks," says Serpell. "An awful lot of dogs don't seem to have much of a self-protective mechanism." When tiny, ancient Ginger attacked the schizophrenic, for example, she did not know that he could hurt her. Tiree had no sense that she could crash through ice when she inched, spread-eagle, toward Jim Gilchrist.

Pack instincts may also explain dogs' risk taking, one scientist believes. As lower-ranking pack members, their brain is hard-wired to know that they are expendable. Instinctively, they also know that keeping higher-ranking members alive is more important than saving themselves. For the good of his "pack," not of the

250 • *In Spite of the Kindness*

person he loved, Klutz fought the rattlesnake, Yogi attacked the rapist, and Ringo threw his body at the fenders of oncoming cars. Max, according to this argument, died protecting Charlotte Bradley after her house exploded only because the dog knew instinctively that his life was less important than hers.

———————

I FIND these arguments impossible to believe. Again and again, the actions of animals themselves contradict what researchers say about them. If we only open our eyes and *look* at animals' kind deeds, we can't deny the caring and concern behind them. We also can't help but see that the scientific emperor is naked, and that many scientists want to believe animals have no feelings and, therefore, cannot suffer. Many researchers "have a vested interest in the position that animals don't feel [compassion or any other emotion]," says James Serpell, "because [those researchers] are using animals in unpleasant ways."

My purpose in this book is not to argue; by their own actions described in the stories I collected here, the animals, I feel, would win any debate. Nevertheless, rather than arguing, I want simply to appeal to common sense. Apply it, for instance, to the three scientific theories that interpret animals' kindness as selfishness; those theories can just as easily explain away *human* compassion as self-interest. People are usually most compassionate to their own families. Gene selection?

Perhaps. People also engage in reciprocal altruism: Like a zebra picking fleas off another zebra, a mother baby-sits for a friend's child and fully expects the favor to be returned. With pseudo-reciprocity, that mother might take a loaf of pumpkin bread to welcome a new neighbor—and improve her own life by having someone to call for help in emergencies or to pick up mail when she leaves town.

Though we often do carry out these self-interested, "false" acts of altruism, we are also capable of true compassion; we care about others and try to help them without expecting something in return. Surely common sense tells us to give animals credit for this same genuine concern for others that we attribute to ourselves. We would be arrogant to assume that we have a monopoly on kindness.

Yet most scientists ignore common sense and still refuse to give animals the benefit of the doubt for having compassion—or any other emotion. Experts stressed that all the stories I had collected did not provide enough evidence to conclude that concern for others motivated animals to help their human families, strangers, or other animals. As Bonnie Beaver puts it, "Until we actually ask an animal and have it tell us in words we understand [what it feels and thinks], we'll never know."

———

BUT ANIMALS *do* tell of their compassion, not in words, but in deeds. Their actions speak louder than words ever could. If we filter all the anecdotal evidence through common sense, we can scarcely *not* believe that animals are truly and profoundly compassionate. To arrive at the truth, we must trust our own eyes and ears.

Weela, a pit bull in Imperial Beach, California, just north of the Mexican border, can tell us more about animal kindness than any scientific theory. She has helped so many animals and people in so many ways for so many years that no one could deny her kindness. . . .

Lori Watkins was not pleased when her aunt arrived with five pit bull pups that she'd rescued from a garbage can. Although the pups yipped and squirmed with life, they were also sick and not especially attractive. Probably for these reasons, the pups had literally been thrown away, Lori figured; she was too kind not to take them in.

Unfortunately, one pup died, but she nursed the others back to health and found homes for three of them. The fourth, Weela, a plain, red-orange creature, became so attached to Lori's eight-year-old son Gary that he pleaded to keep her, and Lori gave in.

A few months later, Gary and his best friend were playing in the street with Weela on a leash. A neighborhood bully stopped the boys, squirted lighter fluid on them, and tried to set them on fire with a match. While fighting to defend himself, Gary accidentally let go of Weela's leash. She jumped on the bully and knocked him down until Gary and his friend could run away.

Not long after that, Gary reached down to pick up what he thought was a lizard in a woodpile. Weela leaped in front of him, hit him in the knees, and shoved him back. She had jumped into the path of a rattlesnake that was about to strike Gary's knees. Instead, the rattlesnake bit Weela in the face. Though the boy was safe, Weela's head ballooned up so much that her air passages almost swelled shut. She spent many painful days recovering.

Three years later, heavy rainstorms flooded the Tijuana River in the valley where the Watkinses lived. The normally shallow, narrow river turned into a raging torrent and endangered the horse and seven dogs of Lori's friend Paul, who was hospitalized. One evening Lori and her cousin Carol Kaspar drove with Weela to Paul's ranch. After slogging through waist-high water, they found his stranded animals; but when they started back to dry ground, the water had risen too high to cross.

Splashing around nearby, Weela showed Lori and Carol that she'd found a shallow crossing place. With her head lowered to hear the river currents, she nosed along embankments, fallen tree trunks, and other submerged high places and led Lori and Carol back and forth across the water to save Paul's animals.

A week later when the river was flooding even worse than before, Lori and Carol found fifteen horses and four dogs stranded on an island of manure, mulch, and sand that could wash away at any moment. Again, Weela led Lori and Carol along the most expedient route, kept them from drowning, *and* prevented them from stepping on hidden barbed-wire fences, quicksand, and mud bogs. Working together, Weela, Lori, and Carol managed to get the horses to safety.

The four stranded dogs, however, were so frightened and wild that they would not let anyone approach them. Since Lori and Carol could not lead them off the island, the women brought food to them instead. Day after day for several weeks, Weela—with a fifty-pound pack of dog food strapped to her back—led Lori and Carol across the river to the dogs until they became tame enough to be rescued. Lori tethered one of them to Weela, who swam with him to shore. Then Weela led Lori and Carol through shallow places across the river with the other three dogs.

A few weeks later, officials across the border opened the Rodriguez Dam without warning, and the valley flooded yet again. As Lori and Carol were digging a horse trailer out of the sand, thirty Mexican aliens ran past them and Weela toward a dangerous part of the river. The aliens prepared to cross.

"Stop! Stop! You'll drown!" Lori shouted.

Not understanding English, the Mexicans waded farther into the river.

"Dangerous water!" Lori tried again. "*Peligro agua!*"

More frightened of her than of the river, the Mexicans ran downstream. Just as they were about to start to the other side, Weela charged toward them, barked, snarled, and kept them from crossing until Lori could reach them. She gestured for them to form a chain by holding hands. With great care, Weela slowly led the group to places that were only knee-deep, where they could cross the dangerous currents.

Helping so many people and animals in the floods over so many weeks changed Weela from a carefree pet to a worker with a mission. The greatest proof of her metamorphosis: After the floods when she had no useful work to do, Weela became lethargic, lay around all day, and moped.

"I feel so guilty," Lori told her husband, Daniel. "We let Weela do so much in the floods, and now we're abandoning her to sit around and get depressed. She needs something to do."

If Weela wasn't actively helping people, Lori concluded, the dog would always be listless and bored. So Weela took on a new career as a therapy dog. Every Tuesday, she and Lori went to Alvarado Hospital to visit patients. The pit bull snuggled up to anyone who needed reassurance, jumped and waved her paws at anyone who needed to laugh. If patients wanted to talk with Lori about their own dog or their problems, Weela sat quietly in a chair and did not bother them.

"She senses everybody's needs," Lori told Daniel.

She also intuitively sensed the needs of other animals. Someone brought the Watkinses a sick and semiconscious yellow pit bull puppy named Chloe, who had a heart murmur and a wounded leg. Weela cuddled up to her and licked her fur clean. As the pup's leg began to heal, Weela massaged it with her tongue, nosed Chloe around the yard, and made her exercise her muscles.

After Chloe recovered, a friend brought Lori a silver-gray potbellied piglet, just twenty hours old. Weela curled her body around him and wouldn't let any of the family's other pets come near. As the pig got older and began wandering around, she would not let him go to the yard alone. She followed him outside and protected him until he grew into a hefty pig, named Graystoke, and Lori's son Gary took the two animals to visit classes of mentally disturbed children. Then Weela would get busy entertaining the kids.

In spite of Weela's exemplary record as a champion of animals and people, Lori continually had to battle prejudices against pit bulls. Wherever she took Weela, Lori was bombarded with ignorant questions:

"How can you *stand* having a pit bull?"

"Isn't that a horrible dog?"

"Aren't you afraid that dog is going to turn on you?"

Lori often simply responded that "every animal is a reflection of its owner." Weela and Lori reflected each other's concern for anyone in trouble.

As Weela has carried out her mission of helping year after year, she has been a model of compassion, not just for other animals, but for people, too. Instead of labeling Weela a vicious, nasty animal, many people might call her an angel.

———

AT LEAST half the people I interviewed for this book told me, "My pet was an angel!" Without my asking questions to draw out this response, again and again people insisted that their animals had carried out the duties that angels are supposed to perform in the service of God. The creatures had delivered messages and warned of danger. The animals had guarded, protected, comforted, encouraged, and rescued people. God had put the animals, willing to help, in just the right place at just the right time, many people believed. The creatures had been angels in fur.

Whether or not we believe in angels seems less important than acknowledging Weela's and other animals' compassion. They reveal it constantly and in so many different ways—if we will only *see* it. Sometimes animals seem to have been put on the earth for the specific purpose of caring about us and helping us. They are powerful forces for good.

AFTERWORD

I AM ALWAYS collecting stories of animal compassion. If you know a creature that has been kind in some way and you would like to share that experience with me, please send your story to Kristin von Kreisler, c/o Prima Publishing, 3875 Atherton Road, Rocklin, California 95765. If possible, please include your address or phone number, so I can contact you.

Suggested Reading

Bradford, Karleen. *Animal Heroes.* Ontario: Scholastic Canada Ltd., 1995.

Masson, Jeffrey Moussaieff. *Dogs Never Lie About Love.* New York: Random House, 1997.

Masson, Jeffrey Moussaieff, and Susan McCarthy. *When Elephants Weep.* New York: Delacorte, 1995.

McElroy, Susan Chernak. *Animals as Teachers and Healers.* New York: Ballantine, 1997.

Roberts, Yvonne. *Animal Heroes.* London: Pelham Books/Stephen Greene Press, 1990.

Simons, Paul. *Pet Heroes: Amazing Tales of Animal Achievements.* London: Orion Books Ltd., 1996.

Wels, Byron G. *Animal Heroes.* New York: MacMillan Publishing Company, Inc., 1979.

8/98 ⑦